Margarita TIME

Margarita TIME

60+ TEQUILA & MEZCAL
COCKTAILS, SERVED UP,
OVER & BLENDED

CAROLINE PARDILLA

Photographs by Leela Cyd

TEN SPEED PRESS
California | New York

CONTENTS

INTRODUCTION 1
WHERE TO BEGIN 9

STARTING SIMPLE

Classic Margarita 28

Tommy's Margarita 30
by Julio Bermejo

Adiós Margarita 31
by José Medina Camacho

Lonesome Rose Margarita 32
by Paul McGee and Julia McKinley

Gram-arita Cadillac
Margarita Batch 35
by Eric and Jean Michel Alperin

Frozen Margarita 36
by Travis Tober

Madre Mezcal Margarita 37
by Ivan Vasquez

Hibiscus Margarita 38
by Shannon Mustipher

Ranch Water 40
by Kevin Williamson

Lagerita 41
by Simon Ford

Smells Like Teen Spirit 42
by John deBary

50/50 Margarita* 45
by Natasha Bermudez

MARG MASH-UPS

Mexican Martini 48
by Ellen Kruce

Retox 49
by Sother Teague

Dirty Marg-tini 51
*by Demi Close and
Jazzton Rodriguez*

Sí Punch 52
by Max Reis

Hail Mary 54
by Daniel Eun

Oaxacan Sunrise 56
by Emily Mistell

Foolish Pleasures 59
by Kevin Diedrich

Baller's Margarita 60
by Erick Castro

BLENDED RENDITIONS

Boogie Nights 64
by Vince Ott

Tommy's Amontillado 67
by Paul Taylor and Sherra Kurtz

Frozen Jägerita 68
by David Cordoba

Booker & Dax Blender
Margarita 69
by Dave Arnold

Summer Melon Marg 71
by Andrew Burton

FRUITY RIFFS

Mano a Mango 74
by Lynnette Marrero

Waterloo Watermelon
Margarita 77
by Justin Lavenue

Super Strawberry Margarita 78
by Trevor Easter and Britta Currie

Black Forest Margarita* 80
by Kim Haasarud

Coconut Margarita 81
by Beau du Bois

Hang Loose Brah 83
by Christine Wiseman

The Day After the Day
of the Dead 84
by Matthew Biancaniello

VEGGIE VARIATIONS

Red Zeppelin 89
by Abigail Smith

Bruce Banner 90
by Julian Cox

Podracer 92
by Stuart Weaver

Low Altitude* 93
by Natasha David

Spa Day Margarita 95
by Chris Bostick

Margarita Verde 96
by Stacey Swenson

SPICY SELECTIONS

Margarita Toreada 100
by Bricia Lopez

El Morado* 101
by Gaby Mlynarczyk

Picante Amante 102
by John Hardin

Christmas Margarita 105
by Natalie Bovis

Malcriada 106
by Christian Suzuki-Orellana

Sonámbula 109
by Ivy Mix

**Maison Margarita
de Jamaica 110**
by William Elliott

Margarita Al Pastor 113
by Benjamin Padrón

Georgia O'Keeffe 114
by Jen Len

28 Guava Spicy Margarita 117
*by the team at
28 HongKong Street*

CRAFTY TAKES

Vast Acid Margarita 121
by Chockie Tom

Mano de Chango 122
by Kim Stodel

BLT Margarita 124
by Sarah Crowl

Southbound Suarez 126
*by Jeffrey Morgenthaler and
Benjamin Amberg*

Hocus Pocus 127
by Danielle Crouch and Allan Katz

Big River 128
by Christiaan Röllich

Clarified Margarita 131
by Max Reis

Baby Turtle 132
by the Team at Trick Dog

Dat Purple Marg 135
by Ramsey Musk

Marguerite* 136
by Adam Fournier

ICONIC ITERATIONS

Primo Margarita 141
by Tony Abou-Ganim

Salt Air Margarita 142
by Chef José Andrés

The Infante 145
by Giuseppe González

Rhode Island Red 146
by Vincenzo Marianella

SYRUPS, SUPER JUICE,
AND SALTS 149
ACKNOWLEDGMENTS 150
INDEX 152

*Low-ABV or nonalcoholic recipe

FOR THE HARDWORKING PEOPLE
WHO POUR THEIR SOULS INTO
MAKING TEQUILA

INTRODUCTION

When I first started drinking in my twenties in Los Angeles, my only encounters with the margarita were during happy hours, backyard parties, and Cinco de Mayo. Back then, I wasn't much of a drinker. Cocktails weren't meant to be enjoyed but were rather a means to a buzz. As a result, I thought the margarita came in two forms: a not-very-good drink with a heavily salted rim or a sweet slushy. It wasn't until I became enamored by the cocktail scene—at the start of the cocktail renaissance in the early 2000s—and ended up blogging about it, that I finally experienced a well-made classic margarita. My mind was blown.

Cut to a couple of decades later—I can generally get a read on someone by the type of margarita they favor. If their go-to is a Tommy's Margarita, odds are good that they're an expert-level imbiber who enjoys the nuances of the spirit. If it's a frozen strawberry margarita they're after, they're not too keen about the taste of tequila or their catchphrase is "It's five o'clock somewhere!" (I started out the latter and am now the former.) For fun, I like to apply the same character assessment to which margarita origin story they gravitate toward. There are lots.

Unlike many classic cocktails, the margarita has people from all over claiming to have invented it. Most of those creation myths typically involve a remarkable woman for whom the drink was named. For silver screen lovers, there's the story of the cocktail being created in honor of movie star Rita Hayworth when, as a teenager (née Margarita Cansino) during the '30s, she performed at Agua Caliente Racetrack in Tijuana.

Fans of next-level hospitality will lean toward the canard about Carlos "Danny" Herrera, owner of Tijuana restaurant Rancho La Gloria, who, in 1938, supposedly created the cocktail for Ziegfeld Follies showgirl Marjorie King. This tale, given credence by Herrera's 1992 obituary in the *Los Angeles Times,* tells that Marjorie was "allergic" to all hard liquor except, inexplicably, tequila. However, since she wasn't a fan of the spirit, Herrera disguised its flavor with Cointreau, lemon juice, and salt.

Those who appreciate quick thinking and ingenuity will go for the story set in a bar called Tommy's Place on the Mexican-American border. There, in 1942, the drink spontaneously came about because a bartender named Pancho Morales was too embarrassed to admit he didn't know how to make the Magnolia cocktail a customer requested. He threw together the "juice of one lime, four-fifths tequila, one-fifth Cointreau, salt outside rim of three-ounce glass." Even though it wasn't what the customer ordered, "pretty soon she ordered another one and someone said, 'Hey, what's that?'" Morales mused.

Meanwhile, influencers and jet-setters will see themselves in the yarn about Texas socialite Margaret "Margarita" Sames. Her account in a 1953 *Esquire* article describing her invention—said to have been created during an Acapulco vacation—garnered the first printed mention of the margarita. The Cointreau brand has long sold this story, even quoting her as saying, "A margarita without Cointreau is not worth its salt." According to the lore, Margarita simply wanted a day-friendly cocktail to enjoy by the pool and share with her famous pals, such as Lana Turner and John Wayne. But some credit her friend Conrad "Nicky" Hilton Jr., son of hotel magnate Conrad Hilton Sr., with spreading the recipe by serving it at the Hilton hotels around the world.

The most probable explanation of the margarita's genesis was conveyed by esteemed cocktail historian David Wondrich, who wrote about its history for Patrón's website in 2020. "It's perfectly possible that several different people legitimately invented the Margarita," he writes. "In other words, they may all have been right."

During Prohibition, Americans who headed to Mexico, whether to work as bartenders or simply to drink booze, became acquainted with tequila. And since the Daisy cocktail—made with a spirit, liqueur, and citrus juice—was a standard bar drink around that time, of course tequila would find its way into the mix. "Margarita," which is Spanish for "daisy," really ramped up in popularity around the '50s and '60s. In 1953, the margarita was so beloved that *Esquire* named it December's "Drink of the Month," writing "She's from Mexico, Señores . . . and she is lovely to look at, exciting and provocative." Why *Esquire* chose the coldest month of the year to spotlight this chilly, refreshing tequila cocktail remains a mystery.

No matter how the margarita came about or is made, it garners near-universal appreciation. Celebrants and cocktail lovers reliably adore it, sure, but you'd be hard-pressed to find any drinker who would turn one down, especially on a hot day. Whether serious drinker or occasional tippler, tequila connoisseur or tequila agnostic, they'll say, "Gimme."

WRITINGS

Nathaniel Benchley

Ray Bradbury

Erskine Caldwell

Albert Camus

Joyce Cary

A. E. Coppard

Aldous Huxley

Charles Jackson

Gerald Kersh

Alexander Kirkland

Merle Miller

Liam O'Flaherty

Budd Schulberg

H. Allen Smith

Frederic Wakeman

Evelyn Waugh

Percival Wilde

Ira Wolfert

GRAPHICS

Howard Baer

E. Simms Cam

Eldon Dedin

John Gro

Joel La

Rob

H

The classic margarita has long dominated as America's favorite cocktail—for happy hour, brunch, backyard barbecues, big game Sundays, #MargaritaMonday, and Taco Tuesday—basically any time one is feeling festive. In 2024, it was the third best-selling classic cocktail in the world (behind the Old-Fashioned and Negroni), according to *Drinks International*'s poll of the world's best bars. It was also the top-selling tequila cocktail.

A marg can be found just about anywhere cocktails are served, from roadside cantinas to the world's best bars—a good thing since people seem to crave them wherever they are. At James Beard Award–winning bar Maison Premiere, an elegant New Orleans–inspired oyster and absinthe bar and restaurant in Brooklyn, the classic margarita is always among the top five most-requested drinks. And it isn't even on the menu! Once I saw someone order a marg at The Musso & Frank Grill in Hollywood, a famous century-old steakhouse best known for its martinis.

Certain cities—from Scottsdale, Arizona, to Kansas City, Missouri—have capitalized on the cocktail's popularity, organizing taco and margarita tours to showcase their local bars and restaurants. Dallas mapped out the "best margaritas" for its "Margarita Mile," while Santa Fe, New Mexico, boasts a Margarita Trail complete with an app to guide you along.

The simple but irresistible mix of tequila, orange liqueur, and lime juice is liquid sunshine and fuel for festivities. In 1976, Jimmy Buffett downed a couple of margaritas during a hot day in Austin and then wrote the song "Margaritaville." (His go-to specs: 2 ounces aged tequila, 1 ounce triple sec, 1½ ounces fresh lime juice, 1½ ounces water, and 1 tablespoon superfine sugar.) He unwittingly penned what became a vacation anthem and launched a billion-dollar lifestyle brand for those who never want to leave that blissful "tropical vacation" state of mind. The cocktail is a unifying elixir, symbolizing not just a good time but a damn good time.

This enduring legacy of fun helped make the margarita the second most popular cocktail in the United States during those early days of the pandemic in 2020, coming in just behind the mimosa. "People don't always search out new experiences and emotions," according to Alex Miller, founder and CEO of Upgraded Points, who conducted the analysis. "They want to re-create the feelings of good times that they have already had and fondly remember."

Those who wanted to enjoy their favorite cocktail in the great outdoors when the world's celebrations turned inward during the lockdowns could grab canned margaritas, launching the ready-to-drink category's popularity. Booming sales of margaritas to go were instrumental in helping bars and restaurants stay afloat. "The longer the pandemic went, the larger the to-go margaritas people seemed to crave," wrote Heather Murphy for the *New York Times* in 2021. "Many of the owners of surviving businesses embraced to-go cocktails rapidly and whole-heartedly." Demand has spilled over into the margarita mix market, too, which has evolved considerably since the days of Jose Cuervo "Classic Lime" Margarita Mix. There are enough quality mixes (see page 16) that the category now has online ranking lists on the *New York Times* and Liquor.com.

The well-loved margarita is "almost impossible to make wrong," insists Erick Castro, co-owner of San Diego's acclaimed Raised by Wolves, creator of the modern classic Piña Verde, and a die-hard margarita fan. You can even go to a sports bar, swap out the fresh lime and orange liqueur for sour mix and a splash of orange juice, and still be happy to have a marg in hand, he adds. "It's not Attaboy status [Sam Ross's renowned New York bar] or anything. But it's like, 'Tequila, lime, orange liqueur; I love it.'" The belief here is that because of its forgiving and simple recipe, one that itself is a variation of a classic cocktail, it's easy to riff on with abandon.

And bartenders have done so for decades. In 1971, Dallas restaurateur Mariano Martinez wanted to create large batches of frozen margaritas that were consistently delicious. Blenders weren't cutting it. Customers complained. So, he added loads of sugar to his father's margarita recipe and ran it through an old soft-serve ice cream maker he modified, thus creating the world's first frozen margarita machine.

About fifteen years later, Julio Bermejo of Tommy's Mexican Restaurant in San Francisco decided to showcase the tequila in the cocktail instead of hiding it behind orange liqueur. This move was unthinkable at a time when, according to Bermejo, certain orange liqueur companies pitched their product on its ability to hide the taste of tequila. (Granted, the quality of the tequila at that time was nowhere near what it is today.) Bermejo's variation, the Tommy's Margarita, skyrocketed to success, boosted and given cred by influential local bartender Tony Abou-Ganim, who first tasted it in the mid-'90s. Bermejo's creation hit legendary status and became the preferred margarita of tequila connoisseurs and the cocktail responsible for elevating tequila. In his 1999 article for the *Wall Street Journal,* journalist Jonathan Friedland credited Tommy's Mexican Restaurant as being the epicenter of tequila's revival.

Fast-forward to the cocktail renaissance of the early 2000s, when bartenders revisited classic cocktails. Taking their cues from cocktail legend Dale DeGroff in the 1990s, they pivoted to fresh ingredients and quality spirits. These moves rescued many classic cocktails from being irretrievably lost to crummy bottled juices and cheap liqueurs. Soon, that interest in farmers' market fresh produce brought drink makers into the kitchen, where they adopted chefs' technologies and techniques. The result? An explosion of iterations inspired by the margarita, from modern classic contenders to over-the-top takes. Some riffs involve infusing the spirit with flavors and/or switching up the sweetener, where it's still recognizable as a margarita. Others push the boundaries more forcefully, swapping the tequila for a different agave spirit altogether or changing its form entirely. Some of these interpretations are arguably on the brink of "margarita adjacent," but they only underscore the margarita's inherent versatility.

However, I can confirm that, yes, the margarita actually is easy to screw up, whether with a poor-quality ingredient or too many ingredients. "There's room for error and it's harder to balance," says Ivy Mix, bar owner and author of *Spirits of Latin America*. Also, if the cocktail has anything other than the traditional trio of tequila, lime, and orange liqueur, do not call it a margarita, says Ivan Vasquez, owner of Los Angeles's Madre restaurant, which boasts an impressive mezcal collection of 400 varieties. "Once you add flavors like ginger or pineapple, you distract from the classic margarita," he explains.

That's where this book comes in. It celebrates the margarita in all its forms, from the classic recipe to the frozen slushy to variations demonstrating how this simple tequila cocktail has evolved in the hands and imaginations of today's bartenders. There are even recipes for those who want to take it easy with zero-alcohol as well as low-proof margaritas. Some cocktails here may not technically count as a margarita, but they evoke its spirit. For fun, I also asked the contributing bartenders and drink creators for the margarita specs that they'd make for themselves, including which tequila is their favorite. Everyone has their go-to. Fascinatingly enough, no two recipes are alike, and this speaks to how each values the margarita as an experience. Vince Ott of New York's Thai Diner is a big fan of the sparkling margarita, topping his marg with Topo Chico. Kim Haasarud, author of *101 Margaritas,* rarely makes only one at a time. So, whereas most of the recipes in this book are for one serving, hers is for two!

In this book, I wanted to include recipes created by established drink makers from revered restaurants and bars, with easy, non-fussy steps and readily accessible ingredients (that can be found in most stores and/or ordered online). These criteria, which I picked up from working at *Imbibe* magazine, are important to me as they invite anyone anywhere to make these drinks. And you don't need a fully stocked bar or bartending expertise to try them out. If anything, you may feel emboldened to

experiment with creating your own riffs. *Margarita Time* will equip you with everything you need—from bar tools to proper glassware to recommended tequilas and mezcals—to make delicious margs at home. For those who want to stretch their bartending skills, I even included a few intermediate-level recipes. Hello, Clarified Margarita (page 131)!

This is for you, the margarita lover, the cocktail enthusiast, the agave spirit aficionado. Informed by some of the best bartenders today, *Margarita Time* is a road map to accessible, well-crafted cocktails that can be made in your kitchen or backyard or, really, anywhere you want one. Mix up a batch to toast a birthday blowout with friends or even shake one up for a quiet night in after a long week.

WHERE TO BEGIN

"You can use the best tequila in the world, but when you use a crappy mixer and a cheap triple sec, you bring the integrity of that margarita down to the least common denominator, and the tequila gets lost."

—TONY ABOU-GANIM, THE MODERN MIXOLOGIST
AND PRIMO MARGARITA CREATOR

Even though the margarita seems simple to make with only three key ingredients, amazingly it's also easy to get wrong. Fortunately, if you just stick to balanced proportions and quality ingredients, a tasty margarita is in your future. Here's all you need.

TEQUILAS

Which tequila to use? That's easy. Use your favorite. However, if you don't have one and aren't all that conversant with the spirit, the pro tip is to go with a tequila that's 100 percent agave and additive free (see page 10). That rules out those celebrity tequilas that continue to proliferate on liquor store shelves.

It also excludes mixtos. These tequilas are mixes of 51 percent blue agave and 49 percent sugars. Mixtos are commonly used at places that batch margaritas, just for the fact that they're cheaper. This doesn't necessarily mean all mixtos are bad. There are a few out there sweetened with piloncillo (an unrefined Mexican sugar) versus corn syrup and made using traditional methods. For example, according to Grover Sanschagrin of Tequila Matchmaker, El Tequileño's mixto blanco is popular in Mexico for its affordability. "But it's done in an artisanal way," he says. "Everything is small batch and traditional in their process" versus rapid and industrialized methods. But since a mixto's sweetener masks the agave flavors, using one doesn't do the margarita any favors.

Celebrated bartender and Modern Mixologist Tony Abou-Ganim said that while mixtos had turned him off all tequila as a young bartender, it was his first taste of a 100 percent blue agave blanco in 1985 that opened his eyes to the true beauty of the spirit.

Don't feel bad if you're overwhelmed by the sheer breadth of the tequila category. Tequila's explosion in popularity means there are more great choices than ever. You can simplify the research process by using the website Tequila Matchmaker (tequilamatchmaker.com), which rates tequilas and features a comprehensive list of additive-free tequilas. Tequila Matchmaker also has an app for easy reference. This is so helpful when you're facing a wall of bottles at the liquor store and need a quick but tested recommendation.

In this book, most bartenders specify which brand of tequila they use in their margarita-inspired recipes. But for the traditional recipe, the choice of tequila hinges on the type of margarita you want. Do you want a light thirst quencher or something deeper in flavor? There are five classifications of tequila, and all four of them, except extra añejo, are generally mixed into margaritas.

Blanco (aka Plata or Silver): This pristine, agave-forward tequila, which is bottled after it's distilled, is what bartenders most often reach for when making margaritas, purely for the fact that its robust flavors can stand up to the other ingredients in the cocktail. It's bright, grassy, peppery, and especially refreshing on a warm day.

Joven (aka Gold): This category—a blanco mixed with an aged tequila (reposado or añejo)—isn't often considered as an option for mixing in

---

Tequila Terroir

Highlands (Los Altos) Tequila: Tequila produced from agave plants grown in the high-altitude region of Jalisco, Mexico, tend to be sweet and fruity thanks to the iron- and potassium-rich red clay soil. Examples: Siete Leguas, Tapatío, El Tesoro

Lowlands (Los Valles) Tequila: The lowlands agave plant benefits from the mineral-rich soil of the Volcán de Tequila, an inactive volcano near Jalisco, making for an herbaceous and earthy tequila. Examples: Fortaleza, Cascahuín, Siembra Valles

---

margaritas. While a blend of blanco and repo sounds like the best of both worlds—the potency of an unaged tequila with a bit of the richness imparted by a barrel—the reality is that they're usually mixtos and loaded with additives.

Reposado: When a blanco is rested or aged in an oak barrel or steel container for anywhere from two months to a year, its flavors mellow out, making for a smooth marg. The barrel imbues the tequila with a light amber color, and its oakiness imparts notes of vanilla and spice. Tequila aged in ex-bourbon barrels comes out tasting a bit sweet, having adopted the flavors of the whiskey.

Añejo: Some may argue that shaking up a pricey, aged (one to three years) tequila in a margarita is a waste of a perfectly good sipping spirit. Don't believe it. An añejo makes for a smoother and sweeter margarita whose rich, warm notes complement the orange liqueur. But if you want your añejo to shine even more in the cocktail, make a Tommy's Margarita (see page 30), which leaves out the liqueur altogether.

T I P

Additive Free: The Tequila Regulatory Council (Consejo Regulador del Tequila)—a nongovernment body funded by the Mexican government to regulate the tequila industry—allows tequila brands to include additives up to 1 percent of the spirit. As such, some producers add artificial flavors, sugars, coloring, and even glycerin to mask "imperfections" of the product under the guise of "consistency." Mass-produced brands, particularly celebrity-owned ones, taste sweet and smell like cake batter in part because of their additives. It's important to note that just because the bottle says "100% blue agave" doesn't mean it's free of additives.

ACID

Simply put, this is where a margarita can easily go south. The citrus component typically provides the acid, and it pays to do it right.

In the '70s and '80s, bottled sour mix, with its preservatives and artificial sweeteners, was the go-to replacement for lime juice. This substitution ruined the cocktail for generations. It wasn't until legendary bartender Dale DeGroff shined a light on the importance of using fresh juices in cocktails—an epiphany that his disciples, such as Clover Club's Julie Reiner, continued to promote—that the margarita was redeemed.

Here are how modern bartenders are adding acid to their margs, including sustainable options.

Lime juice: Fresh-squeezed lime juice is far and away the best choice in a margarita. Don't bother trying to cheat by using bottled juice or day-old juice unless you want your cocktail to suffer. *Liquid Intelligence* author Dave Arnold tested the taste of lime juice at various ages, from immediately fresh-squeezed to twenty-four hours old, and discovered that "the day-old juice always loses." Compared to grapefruit and lemon, a lime's flavor is the most fragile, changing as soon as the fruit is juiced. But interestingly enough, bartenders such as Arnold and Pacific Standard's Jeffrey Morgenthaler prefer lime juice that's aged a few hours, about four, as it features a nice acidic bite. While bars may squeeze limes before a shift to save time when making the drink for customers, there's no reason a home bartender can't take a minute to cut and squeeze a lime for their cocktail.

Lime cordial: During the dark ages of cocktails—the '70s and '80s—Rose's Lime Juice Cordial was a staple of bad margaritas. Lately, bartenders have been making their own lime cordials using lime zest, fresh lime juice, sugar, and a neutral spirit. A proper homemade one (skip the Rose's) can be used in place of lime juice and sweetener and is convenient when batching margaritas for the masses (see page 110).

T
I
P

Juicing: To get the most juice out of the fruit, according to bartender Jeffrey Morgenthaler, refrigerate it before cutting it. In his 2014 book, *The Bar Book: Elements of Cocktail Technique*, Morgenthaler tested the "roll the fruit to get more juice" theory on lemons, which are structurally similar to limes, and found that simply refrigerating the fruit and not rolling it produced the most juice. Meanwhile, refrigerating the lemon and rolling it resulted in the least. The difference is only about a ½ teaspoon more juice per lemon, but at least refrigerating it will keep the fruit fresher longer and colder, he says.

For juice pressing, cut the fruit in half and make sure to also cut off the ends of it, exposing some of the flesh. Doing so will effectively create an escape path for the juice in the depths of the fruit. This also reduces the effort to squeeze the press and minimizes the chance of a juice explosion. Always place the fruit with the large cut side down in the press so that the juice can easily drain through the holes.

Sūpāsawā: This bottled nonalcoholic super sour mixer—which is made up of malic acid, succinic acid, tartaric acid, citric acid, phosphoric acid, a bit of sugar and salt, and distilled water—has been adopted by bartenders seeking a sustainable alternative to lime juice. It also serves well as a hack for making a clarified cocktail, such as a crystal-clear daiquiri or clarified margarita. Keep in mind, though, that while it does add acidity to the cocktail, it lacks that fresh lime zing.

Super juice: Here's another party-friendly citrus juice alternative that is cheaper than using fresh juice. Super juice (page 149) is made with lemon or lime peels, lemon or lime juice, citric acid, malic acid, and water. This sustainable option created by Nickle Morris of Louisville's Expo can turn 10 to 12 limes into a liter of super juice that lasts up to a couple of weeks in the refrigerator.

ORANGE LIQUEURS

Orange liqueur is a category of orange-flavored distilled spirits consisting of triple sec and curaçao. As the third ingredient of a margarita, its citrusy sweetness counterbalances the tartness of the lime juice and brings a complexity to the drink. Like your tequila, which one you pick will affect the character of the cocktail, either playing up its brightness or giving it some depth.

Triple sec: This category of orange liqueur is traditionally made by steeping dried orange peels in a neutral base spirit. Originating from France in the 1800s, its name translates to "triple dry" in reference to its "more concentrated blend of three separate distillations" and more bitter-orange flavor, according to *The Oxford Companion to Spirits and Cocktails.* However, the category name has gotten a black eye due to the many lesser-quality and artificial-tasting versions on the market. As a consequence, premium brands such as Combier and Cointreau have removed the term from their bottles. But don't let that scare you off from all triple secs as there are many more affordable, non-Cointreau bottles to choose from, such as Giffard, Luxardo, and Marie Brizard.

Cointreau: Said to have been the first one to register the term "triple sec," in 1885, Cointreau also claims to be the liqueur used in the original margarita. Today, it continues to be the preferred orange liqueur for the classic cocktail. It's no coincidence that the majority of recipes in this book use Cointreau. "Out of all the ones I've tried, it pairs the best with agave," says bar owner and author Ivy Mix, adding that it showcases the tequila the best. It also has a higher ABV (alcohol by volume) than most triple secs: 40 percent ABV versus 15 to 20 percent ABV in others.

Combier: Touted as the first triple sec ever made, Combier Liqueur d'Orange was invented by confectioner Jean-Baptiste Combier in 1834 to fill his chocolates. Today the clear orange liqueur is a popular, sweeter, and slightly cheaper alternative to Cointreau in margaritas. Like Cointreau, it's distilled from sugar beets and steeped with dried orange peels.

Grand Marnier: This caramel-colored orange liqueur is 51 percent aged cognac and 49 percent triple sec, making it pricier than Cointreau. With its fuller body and richer flavors, it creates a toasty and more complex margarita versus the bright and refreshing Cointreau margarita. Its flavor profile complements aged tequila well, less so with blanco tequila. It's generally used in a Cadillac Margarita, aka a margarita with premium spirits, as a float or shaken into the cocktail.

Curaçao: Unlike triple sec, which is a clear orange liqueur, curaçao comes in a variety of colors, ranging from clear to blue. Because its base spirit is cognac or brandy versus a neutral spirit, it features warmer and richer flavors than triple sec. The name originates from a time when the liqueur was made from the bitter laraha oranges harvested from Curaçao, the Dutch island near Venezuela. However, since curaçao isn't a protected appellation, it doesn't need to be made from those specific oranges to put the name on its label.

SWEETENERS

The traditional margarita recipe doesn't include a sweetener other than the orange liqueur. But for those who prefer a sweeter marg, sweetener can be added to round out the tartness (from a bar spoon to ¼ ounce).

Agave nectar: The common belief is that agave nectar is superior to simple syrup in a margarita because the nectar plays up the tequila's grassy notes since they're both derived from agave. However, *Liquid Intelligence* author Dave Arnold believes that commonality is just a coincidence. Basically, you "use agave when you don't want the sweetness to linger," he wrote. Note that agave nectar is a more concentrated sweetener than sugar and has a near-honey-like consistency. It's best to either cut it with warm water to make agave syrup (page 149) or use one-quarter to one-half less than you would for simple syrup when mixing it in cocktails.

Grades of Agave Nectar

- **Light:** a mild and neutral-tasting sweetener best used in delicately flavored cocktails
- **Raw:** this mild, neutral-tasting light agave is the least processed and heated at lower temperatures
- **Amber:** a darker and more caramel-flavored grade, which is versatile
- **Dark:** a very rich grade that can stand in for brown sugar or a light molasses

---

Agave syrup: When "agave syrup" is listed in a recipe as an ingredient, it means cutting agave nectar with water, usually 1:1 (see page 149), which makes it easier to mix into a cocktail since it's not as viscous or sweet. Think: mixing water with honey to make a honey syrup. Be aware that the "agave syrup" you see at the store usually contains highly processed agave and high-fructose corn syrup, which lace your cocktail with a synthetic-tasting sweetness.

Simple syrup: If you regularly make cocktails at home, then you're no stranger to using or even making simple syrup. It's simply one part sugar and one part water (see page 149), and its function is to sweeten and balance a cocktail. In a margarita, a plain simple syrup has a neutral sweetness, making for a cleaner-tasting cocktail. Occasionally, a recipe will call for a rich simple syrup, which means adding two parts sugar to one part water (see page 149).

MARGARITA MIXES

Let's face it. When you're hosting a party, you don't want to have to squeeze dozens of limes or be stuck in the kitchen on margarita duty. The flip side is that shortcutting with artificial-tasting mixers is unthinkable. Fortunately, nowadays, enterprising bartenders are crafting mixers that don't skimp on quality and are made with fresh juices. Here are a few worthy of your good tequila. Just set them out on a table with a bottle of tequila, a bucket of ice, and a shaker, and have your party guests help themselves.

Keep in mind that all of these mixes cover the lime and agave sweetener portions of a margarita. They don't include orange liqueur because it would just complicate things for the producers. "[Mixes with orange liqueur] can only be sold with alcohol, which can be seen as limiting

BLENDER TIPS

Slowing down separation: The fear of brain freeze usually prevents us from quickly sucking down a frozen cocktail. We often let the drink sit and carefully sip it. But as it sits, it inevitably begins to separate, looking not so appetizing. Max Reis of Mirate in Los Angeles has a tip to prevent the separation and improve texture. Sure, it entails picking up a couple of things from a store like Modernist Pantry (modernistpantry.com), but once that's done, it's an easy fix. When blending a couple of frozen margaritas (4 ounces blanco tequila, 1½ ounces Cointreau, 2 ounces fresh lime juice, ½ ounce simple syrup), also add ¼ teaspoon xanthan gum and ¼ teaspoon Foam Magic to the blender. Pulse to combine the liquid thoroughly and then drop in 2 cups of ice. For a larger batch, Reis increases the amounts to 1½ teaspoons xanthan gum and 1½ tablespoons Foam Magic to add to 4 gallons of frozen cocktail.

Flavored ice cubes vs. regular ice cubes: Make ice cubes do something for your cocktail other than chill and dilute it. Travis Tober of Nickel City in Austin prefers to make ice cubes with orange pekoe tea for his Frozen Margarita (page 36) to help boost the orange notes of the Cointreau and minimize diluting the flavors. For frozen fruit margaritas, freeze juice in an ice cube tray and use those juicy cubes (or frozen fruit) in place of regular ice cubes when blending the drink.

Blend easy: To avoid creating a watery frozen margarita, go easy on how much ice you add. Start blending on the low setting just to break up the ice and then ramp up the speed to blend until smooth, making sure to not blend for too long.

your distribution points," says Fresh Victor's chief mixology officer H. Joseph Ehrmann, adding that having to source a third-party alcohol supplier would increase costs.

Cheeky Lime Juice and Agave Syrup: The Cheeky lime juice and 3:1 agave syrup are sold in separate bottles, allowing you to dose as you wish. Founded by beverage industry veteran April Wachtel, the company produces juices and syrups using all-natural ingredients. They include no preservatives or artificial flavors or colors. Being the real deal, they do need to be refrigerated as soon as they're opened and will last about a month.

Fresh Victor Mexican Lime & Agave: Add 3 ounces of this mixture of fresh cold-pressed lime juice sweetened with organic cane sugar and agave nectar to a shaker with 1½ to 2 ounces of your favorite blanco or reposado tequila for their "Fresh Agave Margarita." For a classic margarita, Ehrmann recommends adding a couple dashes of orange bitters or a touch of triple sec. "I don't ever add more than ½ to ¾ ounce of an additional sweetener," he says. To really spice up your party, shake up margs with Fresh Victor Jalapeño & Lime mix. It, too, is made with lime juice, cane sugar, and agave nectar but includes jalapeño puree and oleoresin capsicum, a natural pepper extract.

Filthy Margarita Mix: Filthy, by founder Daniel Singer, started out with a focus on creating quality olive and cherry garnishes. It has since expanded to include Bloody Mary, Dirty Martini, and Margarita mixes that are preservative-free and not concentrate. The Margarita Mix, made from 100 percent Florida lime juice and organic agave nectar from Jalisco, comes in a 32-ounce party-ready and travel-friendly pouch that is good for making ten drinks. For each drink, simply add 3 ounces of the mix to 1½ ounces of tequila.

BARWARE

Blender: Whip up a frozen margarita with a blender by adding the ingredients with ice. It'll make for a slushy that you can drink through a straw. The blender can also be used to make an off-the-stove simple syrup (see page 149) that's room temperature and ready to go.

Citrus press: Since fresh juices are key for a delicious cocktail, a citrus hand press is an essential margarita tool. They're available everywhere, coming in a variety of sizes, styles, and prices.

Electric juicer: An electric juicer is only needed when speed and volume are the priorities. They're great for quickly juicing a bunch of limes for batches of party margs that will be enjoyed right away.

═══ SHAKING METHODS ═══

Shake: A simple shake where you add your cocktail ingredients and ice to a shaker and shake for about 15 seconds or until the shaker is frosty.

Shake and dump: Bartenders such as Erick Castro and Kim Stodel recommend this method of shaking your cocktail and then dumping the shaker's entire contents into your glass. Castro calls it the "party dump." Then top with fresh ice, but less than what you'd use for a strained marg. This technique is useful if you're a slow sipper and don't want your drink to become overly diluted.

Regal shake: For this technique, add a grapefruit peel to the shaker with the cocktail ingredients and ice before you shake it. It's a quick and simple way to amplify the citrus notes and complexity of the cocktail. Theo Lieberman, beverage director of Delicious Hospitality in New York, is credited with coming up with the technique in 2010 while he worked at Milk & Honey. Lieberman uses it for the daiquiri and Gold Rush. When dropping a grapefruit peel in a shaker of margarita, he says, "you get super subtle Paloma vibes."

Fine-mesh strainer: To "double strain" or "fine strain," use a fine-mesh strainer in conjunction with the Hawthorne strainer. Doing so prevents ice chips, seeds, and citrus pulp from falling into your cocktail.

Hawthorne strainer: This strainer is meant to be used with shaken cocktails, as opposed to the julep strainer, which is used for stirred drinks. The Hawthorne has a coil that catches large ice chunks.

Shaker: The best shaker is the one you're comfortable using. You can use a Boston shaker (two tins or a tin and a pint glass that fit together), a cobbler shaker (made up of three pieces: a base, a lid with a built-in strainer, and a small cap), or a sealable pitcher for large batches. The right tool for the job also depends on where you're shaking it—backyard party, home bar, or campground—and for how many people.

SPICING UP A MARGARITA

Turn up the heat by adding your preferred spice vehicle to your favorite regular margarita specs. What you choose depends on what type of heat you're going for: something subtle, face-melting, or with a lingering finish. Fiends for fire can even do all of the following.

Muddling or shaking peppers: Add a couple of pepper slices (jalapeño or serrano) to a shaker. You can take out the seeds if you don't want too much spiciness or leave them in for a bit of heat. Muddle the slices and then add the cocktail ingredients along with ice. If you prefer a more subtle heat, skip the muddling and rely on the shaking to squeeze out the flavors. Shake until chilled. Strain into a rimmed glass over ice and garnish with a pepper slice.

Hot sauce: Got a favorite hot sauce? Add a couple of dashes, a bar spoon, or even a tablespoon, depending on your desired spice level.

Spicy tincture: Add a couple of drops of spicy tincture (like store-bought Scrappy's Firewater Habanero Tincture or John Hardin's spicy tincture on page 102) to a shaker, then add the cocktail ingredients along with ice. Shake until chilled. Dump into a rimmed glass and garnish with a pepper slice.

Spicy syrup: Replace the agave syrup with a spicy syrup like Kevin Diedrich's jalapeño agave syrup (page 59).

Infused tequila: Bring the fire by using a chile-infused tequila like Ivy Mix's (page 109) instead of a regular one.

Make sure when infusing to taste test often. "I don't like infusing tequila with chiles because I find the end product less controllable," says Mirate's Reis. "If you over- or under-infuse your spice component into your base spirit, it means a lessening or increase of alcohol content" in the cocktail, he explains.

EXTRA SPICY

If you're a spice fiend, go ahead and layer on the heat by rimming the cocktail glass with one of the options below and/or a chile salt (page 149).

Chamoy: This bold Mexican condiment is a sauce or paste made from pickled fruit, such as apricots and mangoes, dried chiles, lime juice, and salt. There are plenty of chamoy sauces available in Latin grocery stores, but you can also make your own. The sauce is often used to drizzle over fruit like fresh-cut mango or to rim glasses for cocktails.

Tajín: This spicy seasoning by Mexican company Empresas Tajín is made up of dehydrated lime, sea salt, and a blend of grounded árbol, guajillo, and pasilla chiles.

The Margarita Glass

Even though many margarita recipes today, like many of the ones in this book, call for a rocks glass, the margarita does have its own vessel named for it. Resembling an upside-down sombrero, the margarita glass is now often used to serve frozen margaritas and other blended drinks. There is no definitive proof of where and how it originated. However, one story says it got its start when a restaurant in Los Angeles received defective Champagne coupes, ones with the "height extender," and decided to use them for margaritas. While in 1964, Victor Bergeron, aka Trader Vic, served the margarita at his Señor Pico Mexican restaurants in Champagne coupes made from amber Mexican bubble glass—hand-blown vessels with tiny bubbles in the glass.

SALTING THE RIM

What's the deal with salt on the rim of a margarita's glass? The bottom line is that this style of cocktail—a daisy—is garnished with a seasoned rim. It's like a Sidecar that way. But unlike the Sidecar, which gets sugar, the margarita uses salt. The salinity accentuates both the sweetness and savoriness of the cocktail and blunts bitter notes. The type of salt you use depends on which type of margarita flavor profile you're going for. Fortunately, there are plenty of margarita salts available in different flavors. Here are the basics. Keep in mind, if you don't like a salted rim's texture or find it distracting, you can instead add saline solution (page 149) to your shaker with the other ingredients.

T
I
P

Rimming a Glass with Salt: First, wet the outside of the rim by wiping it with a fruit wedge. Use lime, lemon, orange, or even pineapple. Liquid such as water or chamoy can be used, too. Then roll the wet portion of the rim in your choice of salt. When rimming a glass, don't dunk it into the salt. Covering both the inside and outside of the glass leaves no escape from the seasoning. Salt on a glass is meant to counteract the bitterness of the cocktail, not make it salty. Swathe only half the rim, again on the outside edge of the glass, to give yourself options of enjoying your marg with or without salt.

Salt: Kosher salt crystals are larger than those of iodized table salt, which means they won't dissolve as quickly and makes rimming a glass easier. It's also cleaner tasting. Sea salt, which has more delicate flakes and a stronger flavor, would work as well.

Spicy chile salt: While it's easy to find a spicy chile salt on the store shelves and online, you can also make your own, tailoring it to your taste. Mix kosher salt with your choice of chile powder, such as cayenne pepper or chipotle, as in Max Reis's recipe (page 149).

Worm salt: The traditional Oaxacan seasoning, known as "sal de gusano," is made of red or white maguey larvae that feed on agave plants. They're dried, ground up, and mixed with chile and salt. Worm salt balances the margarita's sweetness the same way as kosher salt, but adds a touch of heat, umami, and earthiness. Generally, it's served alongside mezcal with orange slices. Sprinkling the fruit's flesh with the worm salt and nibbling on it between sips of mezcal enhances the spirit's flavors. Try it with a mezcal margarita.

T
I
P

Going Garnish-less: The lime wedge is the standard garnish for the margarita. It's meant to give imbibers the option to tart up the drink to their taste. And many of the recipes here include it. However, I'm of the mind that a lime wedge garnish should be optional, just like a salted rim is. Too many wedges on margaritas get thrown out, unsqueezed. Why waste a lime by wedging it and throwing it away when instead it could have been squeezed into the next cocktail?

PICK YOUR PEPPER DEPENDING ON THE SCOVILLE SCALE

Jalapeño and serrano peppers fall in the middle of "just right" on the Scoville scale, which measures the spiciness of peppers, and these two peppers are generally used to spice up margaritas. But unlike the creators of most spicy margarita recipes, Guelaguetza co-owner Bricia Lopez prefers using serrano chiles (see page 100). "Every time I shop for jalapeños, they tend to not have any flavor ... and serranos are always going to come through," she explains. However, with thousands of chile pepper varieties in existence, you have plenty of opportunities to tailor the cocktail to your desired spice level.

MILD		
	ANAHEIM	600 TO 1,000
	POBLANO	1,000 TO 1,500
	HATCH	1,500 TO 2,500
	JALAPEÑO	2,500 TO 8,000
	SERRANO	10,000 TO 23,000
	CAYENNE	30,000 TO 50,000
	THAI	50,000 TO 100,000
	HABANERO	100,000 TO 350,000
SCORCHING	GHOST PEPPER	855,000 TO 1,041,427

Starting SIMPLE

Classic
MARGARITA

1½ to 2 ounces tequila of choice

¾ to 1 ounce triple sec

¾ to 1 ounce fresh lime juice
(see Tips)

¼ to ½ ounce agave syrup or
simple syrup (page 149; optional)

Lime wedge for rim
(optional for garnish)

Kosher salt for rim

A "good" margarita is highly subjective. Some imbibers prefer the drink tarter, others sweeter; some like blanco tequila for its bright agave notes, while others want the mellowness of an aged tequila. Even the volume of tequila may differ depending on whether you're day drinking or really want to taste that tequila.

As for salt, yes. Whether you salt the rim of your glass, add a pinch to the shaker, or use 2 to 7 drops of saline solution (page 149) in the shaker with the other ingredients, you're going to add salt because it not only mellows the bitterness of the lime juice but also turns up the sweetness. The best way to figure out what works for you is to experiment with different ingredient amounts and a variety of brands. Or, you can try the favorite specs of the drink creators in this book.

Rim a rocks glass with salt and set aside (see page 23). Add the tequila, triple sec, lime juice, and syrup (if using) to a shaker filled with ice and shake for 15 seconds (or until the shaker is frosty). Dump the contents into the prepared glass and add fresh ice. Garnish with a lime wedge, if desired.

TIPS

Let the squeezed lime juice age about 4 hours before using (see page 12).

Prechill your glass in the freezer for at least 30 minutes or fill it with ice and ice water while you make your cocktail.

Add a couple drops of yellow or green Chartreuse to the shaker. "It makes everything better."
—**Dave Arnold**

Add a spent lime hull to the shaker. Shaking it with the ingredients and ice will release the lime oils, elevating the citrus notes.
—**Paul McGee**

Zest lime and lemon over the top of the shaker to brighten the cocktail.
—**Julian Cox**

Tommy's
MARGARITA

BY JULIO BERMEJO FOR
TOMMY'S MEXICAN RESTAURANT
IN SAN FRANCISCO

2 ounces reposado tequila

1 ounce fresh lime juice

½ ounce agave nectar

Lime wedge for garnish

Add the tequila, lime juice, and agave nectar in a shaker filled with ice and shake for 15 seconds. Strain over fresh ice in a rocks glass. Garnish with a lime wedge.

Just when the popularity of pre-made mixers and Margaritaville blenders in the '80s reduced the margarita to a neon-green Slurpee, a San Francisco restaurant rescued the classic cocktail. Initially, Tommy's Mexican Restaurant, a family-owned establishment since 1965, had a basic margarita on the menu. It was made with mixto tequila, sour mix, and simple syrup. (They had long replaced the traditional orange liqueur with simple syrup, which technically breaks the rules of the margarita.) But it wasn't until bartender Julio Bermejo, whose parents owned Tommy's, got behind the bar in the late '80s that the restaurant and its margarita were forever changed. And all it took were three simple tweaks to the house recipe: replace the mixto tequila with 100 percent agave tequila, the sour mix with freshly squeezed lime juice, and the simple syrup with agave nectar. The result was a cocktail that made the tequila sing. Tommy's variant was unusual in those days when drinkers and bartenders preferred to have the spirit masked by the orange liqueur. But a modern classic was born as the tides against tequila turned in its favor and the category blew up.

For his variation, Bermejo prefers reposado tequila, finding that in cold and foggy San Francisco a reposado or añejo "has more length and more finish and gives you more warmth." But for warmer climes, a bright and crisp Highland blanco tequila makes the cocktail even more refreshing. Bermejo prefers not to salt the rim of the glass.

Adiós
MARGARITA

BY JOSÉ MEDINA CAMACHO FOR
ADIÓS IN BIRMINGHAM

1½ ounces reposado tequila

½ ounce orange liqueur,
preferably Naranja

¼ ounce dark overproof rum,
preferably Planteray O.F.T.D.

¾ ounce fresh lime juice

½ ounce 2:1 agave syrup
(page 149)

Lime wedge and kosher salt
for rim

Dehydrated lime wheel for garnish

Within its first year of opening in Birmingham, Alabama, in 2022, Adiós, a CDMX-inspired bar by José Medina Camacho and Jesús Méndez, was named one of the best places to drink tequila in the United States by *Food & Wine*. It might come as a surprise that there are only two margaritas on their menu: the Tommy's and this one, basically the classic serve boosted with overproof rum. The idea came to drink creator Camacho in a dream. "It may sound crazy, but many of my cocktails are inspired by dreams," he says. "But I also like a fuller-body margarita, so I thought why not add overproof rum that could add more texture to an already classic cocktail?"

Rim a double rocks glass with salt and set aside (see page 23). Add the tequila, orange liqueur, rum, lime juice, and agave syrup to a shaker filled with ice and shake for 10 to 15 seconds. Strain over ice in the prepared glass. Garnish with a dehydrated lime wheel.

José's Margarita

"If money wasn't a factor, my specs would be 2 ounces Tequila Ocho Añejo tequila, ¾ ounce fresh lime juice, ¾ ounce 2:1 agave syrup [page 149], and 2 dashes 10 percent saline solution [page 149]."

Lonesome Rose
MARGARITA

BY PAUL MCGEE AND
JULIA MCKINLEY FOR LONESOME
ROSE IN CHICAGO

2 ounces blanco tequila,
preferably Cimarron

¼ ounce dry curaçao,
preferably Pierre Ferrand

¼ ounce Combier
Liqueur d'Orange

1 ounce fresh lime juice,
plus 1 lime hull

¼ ounce Petite Canne
sugar cane syrup

¼ ounce agave nectar

For a more layered take on the classic margarita at Chicago's Tex-Mex restaurant Lonesome Rose, Paul McGee (Lost Lake, Three Dots and a Dash) makes a few tweaks. He uses two different types of orange liqueurs and sweeteners and throws the spent lime shell into the shaker with the ingredients. This technique comes from Trader Vic, who used it in his original Mai Tai recipe. "When shaking with the spent hull, it releases essential lime oils that elevate the bright citrus notes in the cocktail and, in our opinion, transform the drink," McGee explains. "It really does make a difference in taste."

Add all the ingredients to a shaker filled with ice and shake for 10 seconds. Dump the entire contents into a rocks glass. Top with crushed or pebble ice.

Paul's Margarita

Coincidentally, this is a simpler version of the Lonesome Rose recipe: 2 ounces blanco tequila (Cimarron, Cascahuín, Tequila Ocho, or Siembra Valles), ¾ ounce dry curaçao, 1 ounce fresh lime juice, ¼ ounce 2:1 cane syrup, and 1 lime hull.

Gram-arita Cadillac
MARGARITA BATCH

BY ERIC AND JEAN MICHEL ALPERIN
FOR COPPER ROOM IN
YUCCA VALLEY, CALIFORNIA

MAKES 17 COCKTAILS

3¾ cups reposado tequila

1⅝ cups fresh lime juice

5 ounces water

4 ounces organic blue agave syrup

8½ ounces Grand Marnier
for floating

Lime wedges and kosher salt
for rim

Lime wedges for garnish

When brothers Eric and Jean Michel Alperin created a cocktail program for the Yucca Valley Airport bar's latest incarnation, Copper Room (formerly the Red Baron), they included a margarita ode to country rock pioneer Gram Parsons. Legend has it that Parsons was a high-rolling regular at the bar in the early '70s, ordering pitchers of margaritas for himself. His last drink on earth? A margarita.

But the brothers' boozy nod to Parsons couldn't be just a margarita. They decided it had to be the Cadillac Margarita, especially after hearing how Parsons's road manager and assistant stole his body after he died and spirited it away in a Cadillac hearse. "Additionally, since Gram was such a big tipper," says Eric, "he deserved and was probably served the best version that [Red Baron bartender] Tim Bullock knew how to shake up." Copper Room has this margarita on tap, but the Alperins created a batched version for sharing with friends.

Rim rocks glasses with salt and set aside (see page 23). Add the tequila, lime juice, water, and agave syrup to a large pitcher without ice. Stir vigorously for 1 minute. When ready to serve, pour 3 ounces of the batch over ice in each prepared glass, float ½ ounce of Grand Marnier over the top, and garnish with a lime wedge.

The mixture will keep in an airtight container in the refrigerator for 3 days. "It is ideally batched and served the same day, 2 hours after the limes have been juiced," says Jean Michel Alperin.

The Alperin Brothers' Margarita

Mezcal Tommy's Margarita made with Rayu or Del Maguey Vida mezcal.

Frozen
MARGARITA

BY TRAVIS TOBER FOR NICKEL CITY
IN AUSTIN

1½ ounces blanco tequila

½ ounce Cointreau

1 ounce lime juice blend
(recipe follows)

½ ounce 2:1 simple syrup
(page 149)

½ cup iced tea cubes
(recipe follows)

Lime wedge and kosher salt
or Tajín for rim

Dehydrated lime wheel for garnish

Making a frozen margarita is more involved than simply adding the margarita ingredients to a blender with ice. As Mariano Martinez, the inventor of the frozen margarita machine, discovered, one needs to also increase the sweetness factor since the cold temperature and added dilution from the ice mute the flavor. But bartender Travis Tober added another dimension to the blended drink: He replaced the regular ice cubes with ice cubes made out of orange pekoe tea. The flavors of the tea complement the tequila and lime, and the tannins add depth to the cocktail.

Rim a rocks glass with salt or Tajín and set aside (see page 23). Add the tequila, Cointreau, lime juice, simple syrup, and iced tea cubes to a blender and blend on low speed to break up the cubes, about 5 seconds. Increase to high speed and blend until smooth, about 10 seconds. Pour into the prepared glass and garnish with a dehydrated lime wheel.

LIME JUICE BLEND

Combine 3 parts Persian (regular) lime juice with 1 part Key lime juice. (While Persian limes are more readily available and can be used for the entire ounce in this recipe, Tober highly recommends seeking out Key limes. "They help change the pH balance of the drink and make it less acidic," he explains.)

ICED TEA CUBES

Steep a bag of orange pekoe tea (or any high-quality orange tea) in 4 cups of water. Let cool, pour into an ice cube tray, and freeze.

Madre Mezcal
MARGARITA

BY IVAN VASQUEZ FOR MADRE
IN SOUTHERN CALIFORNIA

2 ounces espadin mezcal

½ ounce Alma Tepec Chile
Pasilla Mixe liqueur

¾ ounce fresh lime juice, strained

½ ounce agave syrup (page 149)

Lime wheel for rim and garnish

Sal de gusano (see page 23)
for rim

Ivan Vasquez, Oaxacan-born chef and mezcal expert, is a margarita purist. For him, there are only two margaritas: the traditional margarita and the mezcal margarita. Even though his restaurant menus feature margarita-inspired cocktails, he refuses to call them the "M" word. "Anything else will be a modified margarita," he bristles. "Once you add flavors to it, you gotta call it something else." Vasquez created Madre's mezcal margarita in 2015 for his first location, and unlike cocktail legend Phil Ward's modern classic, Madre's version switches out the orange curaçao for a chile liqueur. "We wanted to use some of the natural smoky flavor, not from the mezcal but from the chiles because the chiles are roasted, and their spice balances the mezcal flavor," he says.

Rim a rocks glass with sal de gusano and set aside (see page 23). Add the mezcal, chile liqueur, lime juice, and agave syrup to a shaker filled with ice and shake for 20 to 30 seconds. Strain into the prepared glass over fresh ice. Garnish with a lime wheel.

Ivan's Margarita

2 ounces Gran Dovejo high-proof blanco tequila, ¾ ounce homemade curaçao (recipe follows), and 1 ounce fresh lime juice. Rim half of a double rocks glass with sal de gusano (see page 23) and set aside. Add all the ingredients to a shaker filled with ice, shake, then strain into the prepared glass over fresh ice. Float with ¾ ounce Grand Marnier.

To make Ivan's homemade curaçao, combine 1½ cups aged brandy and 1½ cups agave syrup and stir. Peel 3 oranges and express each peel (squeeze with peel facing down) over the agave-brandy mixture and drop the peels in. Stir to mix well and allow to infuse for 6 hours. Strain out the peels and store in a sealed glass container, where it will keep for 1 month at room temperature.

Hibiscus
MARGARITA

BY SHANNON MUSTIPHER FOR
GLADY'S IN BROOKLYN

1½ ounces blanco tequila

¼ ounce orange curaçao

¾ ounce hibiscus syrup
(recipe follows)

¾ ounce fresh lime juice

Lime wedge and kosher salt
for rim

Lime wheel for garnish

Winner of the Tales of the Cocktail Pioneer Award and author of *Tiki: Modern Tropical Cocktails,* bartender Shannon Mustipher wanted to create a hibiscus cocktail as a nod to her hometown of Charleston, South Carolina. There, the flowers grow along the coast and are traditionally used to make a red drink or tea, similar to West African bissapp and Caribbean sorrel. Since jamaica (hibiscus) is enjoyed as an agua fresca in Mexico, mixing it with the agave spirit was logical. Now this hibiscus margarita with its tangy, cranberry-like flavors, is her go-to riff on the classic cocktail.

Rim a rocks glass with salt and set in the freezer (see page 23). Add the tequila, curaçao, hibiscus syrup, and lime juice to a shaker filled with ice and shake until chilled. Strain into the chilled, ice-filled rocks glass. Garnish with a lime wheel.

HIBISCUS SYRUP

Add 5 whole cloves and 3 cinnamon sticks to a saucepan over medium-high heat and toast for 15 to 20 seconds. Add ½ cup of dried hibiscus flowers to the pan and stir until aromatic, 30 to 60 seconds. Add 1 quart of simple syrup (page 149) and stir to combine. Simmer for 20 minutes, until the mixture is fragrant and a deep purple-pink color. Remove from the heat and let cool for 1 hour. Once cooled, strain into a sealable container. The syrup will keep in the refrigerator for up to 2 weeks.

Note: This makes a large batch, but it can be used as a nonalcoholic ingredient for a sober-friendly option, such as lengthened by seltzer or water with a splash of lemon.

Shannon's Margarita

2 ounces blanco tequila, ½ ounce Cointreau, ¾ ounce fresh lime juice, and ½ ounce 1:1 agave syrup (page 149). Add all the ingredients to a shaker filled with ice, shake, then strain into a rocks glass rimmed on one side with salt. Garnish with a lime wheel.

Ranch WATER

BY KEVIN WILLIAMSON FOR
RANCH 616 IN AUSTIN

2 ounces reposado tequila

1 ounce orange liqueur

1 ounce fresh lime juice

1 (12-ounce) bottle Topo Chico
sparkling mineral water

Lime wedge for garnish

For decades, lovers of this highball take on the margarita believed it was created by cowboys and ranch hands who were stuck out in the field craving the classic tequila cocktail. But in summer 2021, the *Washington Post* named Kevin Williamson, owner and chef of Austin's Ranch 616, as the cocktail's inventor. By adding ice water to his unfinished margarita, he discovered that not only could he lengthen his cocktail, but doing so made it even more refreshing. When he opened Ranch 616 in 1998, he put "Ranch Water" on the menu. Williamson passed away in December 2021, but his legacy was sealed with obits crediting him as "Ranch Water creator."

Add the tequila, orange liqueur, and lime juice to an ice-filled Collins glass and stir to combine. Top with enough Topo Chico to fill the glass. Garnish with a lime wedge.

LAGERITA

BY SIMON FORD IN LONDON

2 ounces blanco tequila

1 ounce Cointreau

1 ounce fresh lime juice

4 ounces Pacifico Clara

Lime wheel for garnish

The internet credits Simon Ford, consummate martini drinker and the co-founder of Fords Gin, with creating the Lagerita. He's not so sure, though. "There is a chance I am the inventor of the Lagerita," he says. "I just can't remember if I was the first to do it." Ford started making it as a bartender in 2000. "It's one I would take on the road for my bartending talks as it was fun," he adds. As it's a better version of the standard beer margarita, he should claim it. While many beer margarita recipes call for mixing tequila, frozen limeade concentrate, and beer, the Lagerita simply tops a perfectly great margarita cocktail with Pacifico. The light lager boosts the refreshment factor of the classic cocktail. It's brighter and carbonated, making it ideal on a scorching summer day.

Add the tequila, Cointreau, and lime juice to a shaker filled with ice and shake until chilled. Strain into a highball or sling glass filled with fresh ice. Top with the beer and garnish with a lime wheel.

Simon's Margarita

2 ounces blanco tequila, ½ ounce Cointreau, 1 ounce fresh lime juice, ¼ ounce agave syrup (page 149), and a pinch of salt. Add all the ingredients to a shaker filled with ice, shake, then strain over fresh ice into a rocks glass. Garnish with a lime wheel.

Smells Like
TEEN SPIRIT

BY JOHN DEBARY IN
NEW YORK CITY

1¾ ounces reposado tequila

¾ ounce amaretto liqueur

¾ ounce fresh lime juice

½ ounce fresh orange juice

¼ ounce simple syrup (page 149)

Lime wedge for garnish

Drink creator and author of *Saved by the Bellini* John deBary worked at iconic New York speakeasy PDT and the Momofuku restaurant group, both high-profile spots with high-quality cocktails. Yet his playful approach to drinks was always embraced. "Even though PDT was quite structured, there was always a bit of tongue in cheek involved in what we did, and Momofuku was always going for a subversive let's-do-what-everyone-else-isn't vibe," deBary explains. "For me it's like, drinking cocktails is a recreational activity, so it really should be as fun as possible!" This open-mindedness led him to find inspiration from the beloved Olive Garden Italian Margarita. To create a drier and more tart balance, deBary dials back the amaretto and turns up the citrus.

Add the tequila, amaretto, lime and orange juices, and the simple syrup to a shaker filled with ice and shake for 15 seconds. Strain into a rocks glass over a large ice cube or serve up in a chilled coupe. Garnish with a lime wedge.

John's Margarita

"I love the classic margarita spec because it's the template for modified sours like the Sidecar, Cosmopolitan, etc., that I find really useful." 1¾ ounces blanco tequila, ¾ ounce Cointreau, ¾ ounce fresh lime juice, and ¼ ounce agave syrup (page 149) on the rocks with salt.

50/50
MARGARITA

BY NATASHA BERMUDEZ
IN NEW YORK CITY

1 ounce mezcal, preferably Mezcal
Verde Amarás Espadín

1 ounce Manzanilla sherry

½ ounce Cointreau

¾ ounce fresh lime juice

¼ ounce light agave syrup
(page 149)

Lime wedge and sal de gusano
(see page 23) or smoked chile salt
(recipe follows) for rim

During the 2020 COVID-19 shutdowns, Natasha Bermudez's go-to drink during Zoom happy hours was the 50/50 martini. But when the weather warmed up, she craved something a bit more refreshing. As a big fan of sherry, which is a common component in her cocktails, Bermudez, bar director for NYC's The Llama Group, thought its salinity and sophistication were the perfect ways to bring down the alcohol in the cocktail while keeping things lively. "Essentially, I took a Tommy's mezcal margarita and added more salinity and nuttiness with the Manzanilla and Cointreau," she says. The result is a weekday-friendly and sessionable margarita.

Rim a rocks glass with sal de gusano or smoked chile salt and set aside (see page 23). Add the mezcal, sherry, Cointreau, lime juice, and agave syrup to a shaker filled with ice and shake until chilled. Strain into the prepared glass over fresh ice.

SMOKED CHILE SALT

Combine equal parts Tajín, paprika, and salt.

Natasha's Margarita

2 ounces Tapatío blanco, 1 ounce fresh lime juice, and ½ ounce 1:1 light agave syrup (page 149). Add all the ingredients to a shaker filled with ice, shake, then strain over fresh ice into a half-salt-rimmed glass. Garnish with a lime wedge.

Marg

MASH-UPS

Mexican
MARTINI

MARGARITA ✦ DIRTY MARTINI

BY ELLEN KRUCE FOR CEDAR DOOR
IN AUSTIN

2 ounces reposado tequila

1½ ounces Cointreau

1½ ounces fresh lime juice

½ ounce green olive brine

Kosher salt

Lime wedge for rim and garnish

Kosher salt for rim

2 green olives for garnish

Legend has it that in the mid-'80s, bartender Ellen Kruce of Cedar Door, a Tex-Mex restaurant and bar in Austin, was inspired to create this drink after being served a margarita in a martini glass while vacationing in Mexico. But the restaurant's current owner Heather Potts credits Austin barman Jim LeMond—"known for his great storytelling abilities and incredible memory of customers' names"—with putting the briny margarita on the map. While a 2011 *New York Times* piece observed, "Outside of Austin, the Mexican Martini is hardly known," the cocktail suits its environment. Something about its savory combination makes it pair perfectly with carne asada tacos. With regard to creating it at home, Potts says: "Some customers enjoy substituting with a spicy tequila or substituting kosher salt with Tajín." But she insists that, unlike other Mexican Martinis around Austin, Cedar Door does not add orange juice to theirs.

Rim a rocks glass with salt and set aside (see page 23). Add the tequila, Cointreau, lime juice, and green olive brine to a shaker filled with ice, shake for 10 seconds, then strain into the prepared glass. Garnish with a lime wedge and two green olives on a cocktail spear.

RETOX

MARGARITA ✦ MASTER CLEANSE

BY SOTHER TEAGUE FOR
RYE IN BROOKLYN

1½ ounces reposado tequila

¾ ounce fresh lemon juice

½ ounce maple-jalapeño syrup
(recipe follows)

Lemon wedge and sweet spicy salt
for rim (recipe follows)

Lemon wheel for garnish

For his riff on the classic margarita, Sother Teague found inspiration from an unlikely source: the Master Cleanse, aka the infamous lemonade detox diet. This fad diet includes dubious claims that lemonade dosed with maple syrup and cayenne pepper will cleanse bodies and quicken weight loss. Teague, the proprietor of celebrated New York bitters bar Amor y Amargo, host of the award-winning podcast *The Speakeasy,* and author of *Drinks with Friends,* wanted to have fun with it by turning the concept on its head. It doesn't include any health claims. Teague says it's simply "a revitalizing cocktail to be enjoyed at any time of day."

Rim a rocks glass with sweet spicy salt and set aside (see page 23). Add the tequila, lemon juice, and maple-jalapeño syrup to a shaker with ice and shake until chilled. Strain over fresh ice in the prepared glass. Garnish with a lemon wheel dipped in the sweet spicy salt.

MAPLE-JALAPEÑO SYRUP

Puree 1 cup of maple syrup with 1 fresh jalapeño or serrano pepper. Double strain into an airtight container. The syrup will keep in the refrigerator for 3 weeks.

SWEET SPICY SALT

Combine 1 part kosher salt, 1 part sugar, ½ part paprika, and ¼ part cayenne pepper. The salt will keep in an airtight container indefinitely.

Sother's Margarita

2 ounces Pueblo Viejo blanco tequila, ½ ounce Pierre Ferrand dry curaçao, 1 ounce fresh lime juice, and ¼ ounce agave syrup (page 149). "I serve with a half-salted rim, but I prefer mine with salt all around."

Dirty
MARG-TINI

TOMMY'S MARGARITA + DIRTY MARTINI

BY DEMI CLOSE AND JAZZTON
RODRIGUEZ FOR VERY GOOD
DRINKS IN OKLAHOMA CITY

2 ounces blanco tequila

¾ ounce fresh lime juice

¾ ounce green olive brine

¼ ounce agave nectar

¼ ounce high-quality extra-virgin
olive oil

Cut olive and sea salt for rim

3 Castelvetrano olives for garnish

Craft bartenders Demi Close and Jazzton Rodriguez started their cocktail company, Very Good Drinks, in 2020, when cocktails to go and home bartending exploded in popularity due to stay-at-home orders. After moving to Thailand the following year, the duo started sharing their recipes on social media. Their creations are inspired by food culture with a DIY approach. "We love taking everyday ingredients and transforming them into a cocktail much like you would when cooking dinner," Rodriguez explains. They amassed followers with their engaging videos about their travels and "if you can think it, you can drink it" cocktail recipes. Wilder ones include the Chicken Soup Martini and a peanut butter, banana, and jelly Boulevardier. For the Dirty Marg-tini, Rodriguez wanted to re-create Tex-Mex staple, the Mexican Martini (page 48), but do a Tommy's take by leaving out the Cointreau and lean into its savoriness by adding olive oil.

Wipe olive brine from a cut olive on the outside of half the rim of a cocktail glass and then dip the glass in sea salt. Place in a freezer while making the cocktail. Add the tequila, lime juice, olive brine, agave nectar, and olive oil to a shaker filled with ice and shake for about 10 to 15 seconds until chilled. Double strain into the prepared cocktail glass. Garnish with three Castelvetrano olives on a cocktail spear.

Demi and Jazzton's Margarita

"We love a Tommy's!" 2 ounces blanco tequila (Cimarron or Arette), 1 ounce fresh lime juice, ¾ ounce agave nectar, 2 dashes Regans' orange bitters, and flaky sea salt.

Sí
PUNCH

MARGARITA ✦ TI' PUNCH

BY MAX REIS FOR MIRATE
IN LOS ANGELES

1½ ounces high-proof blanco
tequila, preferably Cascahuín 48
or Tapatío 110

1 teaspoon Naranja miel syrup
(recipe follows)

1 quarter-size disk of lime,
including peel, pith, and fruit

Lime wedge and kosher salt
for rim

Max Reis, beverage director of Mirate in Los Angeles, looked to the Ti' Punch for this stirred margarita-inspired cocktail. The room temperature classic cocktail features daiquiri flavors but is spirit-forward and stirred. For his take, he swaps out the rhum agricole for a high-proof blanco tequila, and the cane syrup for a honey syrup mixed with Naranja orange liqueur. "Of course, it's hard to resist adding a salt rim as it makes this very clearly a rendition of a margarita, while salinity also helps balance unchilled cocktails," he explains.

Rim a rocks glass with salt and set aside (see page 23). Squeeze the lime disk over the glass, expressing both the juice and the essential oils from the peel, and drop the disk into the glass. Add the Naranja miel syrup. Using a bar spoon, apply pressure to the lime disk to release more oils within the glass. Add the tequila and stir. Slowly add ice to taste, if desired.

NARANJA MIEL SYRUP

Add 3 parts honey and 1 part Naranja orange liqueur (or Cointreau or Combier) to a bowl and stir to combine. The syrup will keep in the refrigerator for up to 2 months.

Max's Margarita

2 ounces Cascahuín 48 Plata tequila, 1 ounce fresh lime juice, ¾ ounce nogave syrup (recipe follows) or 2:1 agave syrup (page 149). Add all the ingredients to a shaking tin with four standard-size cubes, shake hard, then strain into a half-salt-rimmed glass. Top with ice cubes.

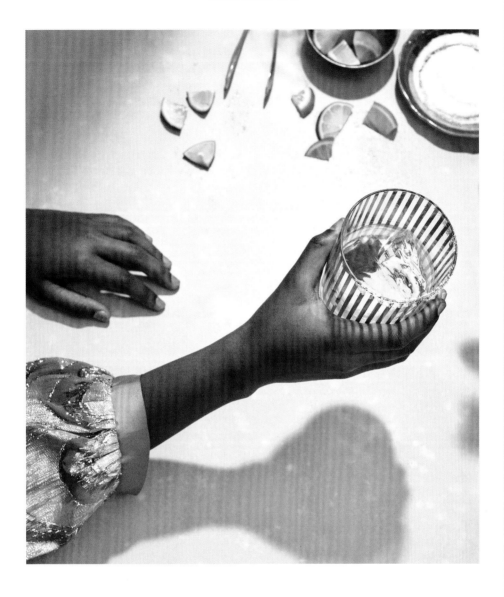

To make Max's nogave syrup, add 3¼ cups hot water to a blender and turn on low, slowly adding 5 cups sugar. When dissolved, add 1½ cups honey and blend until smooth. Store in the refrigerator, where it will keep for 3 months. "I always love a Tommy's, but I make 'nogave' instead because it's less processed and more sustainable and approximates the same flavor," says Reis.

Hail
MARY

MARGARITA ✦ NEW YORK SOUR

BY DANIEL EUN FOR 11 WESTSIDE
IN HONG KONG

1½ ounces blanco tequila,
preferably Cimarron

¾ ounce dry curaçao,
preferably Pierre Ferrand

¾ ounce fresh lime juice

¼ ounce 1:1 simple syrup
(page 149)

Orange wedge

Dry red wine such as Fleurie

Lime wedge for garnish

Daniel Eun was wondering why a float of red wine "wasn't a thing with drinks other than the New York Sour." Eun, who bartended at renowned bars such as NYC's PDT and LA's The Varnish and is now the beverage director for Westside Hospitality in Hong Kong, had this realization in 2015 and put the drink on his menu at 11 Westside in 2017. The float gives the cocktail some berry notes and adds depth. To compensate for the way the wine dries out the drink, he adds a bit more sweetness to his base margarita to restore the cocktail's balance. "It just kind of clicked with the marg. Maybe because we're used to flavored margaritas in general," he says.

Add the tequila, curaçao, lime juice, simple syrup, and orange wedge to a shaker. If you have larger cubes of ice, just shake; for smaller ice, give the orange wedge a quick muddle before shaking. Double strain over fresh ice in a rocks glass. Slowly pour the red wine to layer it on top of the drink. Garnish with a lime wedge.

Daniel's Margarita

2 ounces tequila (Tequila Ocho or Fortaleza), ¾ ounce Cointreau, ¾ ounce fresh lime juice, ¼ ounce 1:1 simple syrup (page 149), and cracked ice or cubes. Add all the ingredients to a shaker filled with ice, give a short, hard shake, then dump into a half-salt-rimmed glass.

Oaxacan
SUNRISE

MARGARITA + TEQUILA SUNRISE

BY EMILY MISTELL FOR HEY LOVE
IN PORTLAND

2 ounces mezcal

½ ounce triple sec

¾ ounce fresh lime juice

½ ounce passion fruit syrup
(recipe follows)

¼ ounce 2:1 simple syrup
(page 149)

2 ounces blended strawberry
margarita for float (recipe follows)

Lime wedge and hibiscus salt
(recipe follows) for rim

Lime wheel for garnish

How does one make a margarita even more fun? By topping it with a float of blended strawberry margarita, which adds more texture and flavor while slowly transforming the drink over the course of enjoying it. Emily Mistell, owner and beverage director of Spirited Awards–winning hotel bar Hey Love, created this eye-catching layered cocktail for Latinx DJ collective Noche Libre. It evokes sipping a Tequila Sunrise while poolside at a Mexican resort. Mistell lowers the strawberry marg slushy's ABV by splitting the tequila amount with rosé, but you can also go all in with 2 full ounces of tequila in the float of strawberry margarita.

Rim a mason jar or a cactus glass with hibiscus salt and set aside (see page 23). Add the mezcal, triple sec, lime juice, passion fruit syrup, and simple syrup to a shaker filled with ice and shake until chilled. Strain into the prepared glass filled with ice. Top with a float of blended strawberry margarita and garnish with a lime wheel.

PASSION FRUIT SYRUP

Add equal parts passion fruit puree, white sugar, and water to a pot over medium-high heat. Stir until fully incorporated. The syrup will keep in an airtight container in the refrigerator for about a month.

BLENDED STRAWBERRY MARGARITA

Add 1 ounce tequila, 1 ounce rosé, ¾ ounce triple sec, ¾ ounce fresh lime juice, ¾ ounce 2:1 simple syrup (page 149), 4 or 5 strawberries, and a scoop of ice to a blender. Blend until smooth.

HIBISCUS SALT

Mix 4 parts kosher salt with 1 part dried hibiscus flowers. Add to a food processor and pulverize. Strain out the unground hibiscus flower parts.

Emily's Margarita

2 ounces blanco tequila, ¾ ounce Giffard triple sec, ¾ ounce lime juice, ¼ ounce agave syrup (page 149), and a pinch of sea salt. "I love a blanco tequila for a margarita. I love Mijenta, Gran Dovejo, Tapatío. Mijenta would be the most approachable of the three, and the other two are a little funkier if you're feeling adventurous."

Foolish PLEASURES

MARGARITA + MAI TAI

BY KEVIN DIEDRICH FOR
PACIFIC COCKTAIL HAVEN IN
SAN FRANCISCO

1¾ ounces honeydew melon and
cucumber–infused blanco tequila
(recipe follows)

¼ ounce overproof rum

¾ ounce fresh lime juice

½ ounce jalapeño agave syrup
(recipe follows)

½ ounce orgeat syrup

1 dash absinthe

Cucumber ribbon plus honeydew
and watermelon balls for garnish

Kevin Diedrich, owner and bartender of Pacific Cocktail Heaven (one of the 50 Best Bars in North America), makes the Mai Tai even more refreshing by crossbreeding it with the margarita. "Margs are crushable, citrusy, and also get tastier as they sit over ice," he explains. To play up the vegetal notes of the blanco tequila, he infused it with summer-ripe honeydew melon and cucumber. A hit of overproof rum, such as Wray & Nephew, makes the cocktail pop while the orgeat's nuttiness and texture round out the drink.

Add the infused tequila, rum, lime juice, jalapeño agave syrup, orgeat syrup, and absinthe to a shaker filled with ice and shake until chilled. Double strain into a double rocks glass over ice. Garnish with a cucumber ribbon and honeydew and watermelon balls.

HONEYDEW MELON AND CUCUMBER–INFUSED BLANCO TEQUILA

Add 3 cups cubed honeydew melon to a 750-milliliter bottle of blanco tequila and let sit for 12 hours. Then add ¾ cup peeled, seeded, and chopped cucumber and let sit for 1 hour. Strain through a fine-mesh strainer. The tequila will keep in the refrigerator for up to 6 weeks.

JALAPEÑO AGAVE SYRUP

Heat 1½ cups agave syrup (page 149) in a pot until simmering. Dice 1 jalapeño, retaining the seeds, and steep in the agave syrup for 3 minutes off the heat. Add all the contents to a blender, blend, and strain out the jalapeño.

Baller's
MARGARITA

MARGARITA ✦ SGROPPINO

BY ERICK CASTRO FOR RAISED BY
WOLVES IN SAN DIEGO

2 ounces Champagne

1 ounce blanco tequila

½ ounce Licor 43

1½ ounces lime sherbet
(recipe follows)

1 cup ice

Orange wedge and kosher salt
for rim

Orange slice for garnish

Erick Castro's love of the Italian sparkling cocktail Sgroppino inspired this margarita. Instead of the traditional lime and agave nectar components, Castro made a lime sherbet using lime juice and peels (peeled before juicing them) left over from the end of the night. "All the cocktail nerds really love the idea of sustainability and reusing ingredients," he says. Meanwhile the addition of Champagne gives the cocktail "this really cool texture," according to Castro, who co-owns one of North America's 50 Best Bars, Raised by Wolves, and hosts the award-winning podcast *Bartender at Large.* Castro says store-bought lime sorbet or sherbet can be substituted, but he highly recommends trying the homemade version. "It's like comparing Chips Ahoy! to homemade chocolate chip cookies."

Rim a hurricane glass with salt and set aside (see page 23). Add the Champagne, tequila, Licor 43, and lime sherbet to a blender and blend with the ice. Pour into the prepared hurricane glass and garnish with an orange slice.

LIME SHERBET

Muddle together 3 cups granulated sugar, ½ cup grated lime zest, and 1½ tablespoons grated orange zest in a bowl. Add 2⅓ cups lime juice, 2 cups water, ¼ cup orange juice, 3 or 4 drops of orange flower water, and ⅔ cup heavy cream and stir to combine. Let the ingredients steep together in the refrigerator for about 1 hour, allowing the citrus oils to properly infuse into the sugar. Strain through a cheesecloth and transfer to an airtight container. The sherbet is ready to use after freezing for 3 to 5 hours. It will keep in an airtight container in the freezer for up to 1 month.

Erick's Margarita

Add 2 ounces blanco, ¾ ounce fresh lime juice, and ¾ ounce agave syrup (page 149) to a shaker filled with ice, shake, then "party pour" (aka dump) in a glass with a salted rim.

Blended

RENDITIONS

Boogie
NIGHTS

FROZEN DRAGON FRUIT MARGARITA

BY VINCE OTT FOR THAI DINER
IN NEW YORK CITY

2 ounces blanco tequila

¾ ounce maraschino liqueur,
preferably Luxardo

¾ ounce fresh lime juice

½ ounce makrut lime simple
syrup (recipe follows)

1 cup ice

1 tablespoon dragon fruit puree
(recipe follows)

Green Chartreuse for spritz

Lime wedge and makrut lime
sugar and salt mix
(recipe follows) for rim

Heads up: Once this herbaceous frozen margarita shows up at a party, everyone will clamor for one. That eye-catching neon magenta swirl of dragon fruit puree is key, adding a pop of color without impacting the drink's flavor. "We really wanted to make it pop and have it sell itself as it travels through the restaurant to the table," explains drink creator and Thai Diner beverage director Vince Ott. "Once a few would go out, they would sell themselves based on looks alone." The Thai-inspired frozen margarita, according to Ott, is more herbaceous than a regular frozen margarita thanks to the makrut lime leaves. That spritz of green Chartreuse (génépy or Strega will work, too) at the end amplifies those aromas.

Rim a rocks glass with makrut lime sugar and salt mix and set in the freezer (see page 23). Add the tequila, maraschino liqueur, lime juice, makrut lime simple syrup, and the ice to a blender and blend until smooth. Add the dragon fruit puree to the prepared glass, then pour in the blended mixture. Spritz the top with green Chartreuse.

MAKRUT LIME SUGAR AND SALT MIX

Add 1 cup plus 2 tablespoons sugar, ⅓ cup plus 1 tablespoon salt, and 2 makrut lime leaves to a food processor. Process until the leaves are broken down. The mixture will keep in an airtight container in the freezer for about 2 months.

DRAGON FRUIT PUREE

Spoon out the fruit from half of a dragon fruit, puree it, and add just enough water (about 1 tablespoon) to thin it out. This puree doesn't store well.

MAKRUT LIME SIMPLE SYRUP

Add 1 cup plus 2 tablespoons sugar, ½ cup water, and 1 or 2 makrut lime leaves to a small saucepan and cook over medium heat, stirring until the sugar has dissolved. Remove from the heat and let cool. Add the mixture to a blender and blend until smooth. Double strain the syrup into a resealable container. It will keep in the refrigerator for 5 days.

Vince's Margarita

2 ounces Cimarron Reposado, ½ ounce Pierre Ferrand dry curaçao, and 1 ounce fresh lime juice. Add all the ingredients to a shaker filled with ice, shake, then pour on rocks. Top with Topo Chico.

Tommy's
AMONTILLADO

FROZEN SHERRY MARGARITA

BY PAUL TAYLOR AND SHERRA
KURTZ FOR COLUMBIA ROOM
IN WASHINGTON, D.C.

2 ounces reposado tequila

1 ounce Amontillado sherry,
preferably Hidalgo "Napoleon"

1½ ounces agave nectar

1½ ounces fresh lime juice

¼ teaspoon 10 percent saline
solution (page 149)

1½ cups ice

Lime wheel for garnish

Paul Taylor and Sherra Kurtz were discussing their love for the Tommy's Margarita when the topic of sherry worked its way into the conversation. It led to an epiphany for the alumni of Washington, D.C.'s now-closed (but still legendary) Columbia Room and owners of sandwich and cocktail bar Your Only Friend: reposado tequila and Amontillado sherry is "a combination that seemed not only right and natural, but perhaps even criminal to *not* at least try," explains Taylor. The sherry "gives a pathway for all the flavors to flow harmoniously with its salinity, acid, and almond-like characteristics," he adds. They turned the drink into a frozen cocktail, doubled the recipe, and increased dilution to refine the texture.

Add the tequila, sherry, agave nectar, lime juice, saline solution, and ice to a blender and blend until smooth. Pour into a tulip glass and garnish with a lime wheel.

Paul's Margarita

1½ ounces Siembra Azul tequila, ¾ ounce agave syrup (page 149), and ¾ ounce fresh lime juice. Wipe the outside of half the rim of a rocks glass with a lime wedge, dip in salt, and set aside. Add all the ingredients to a shaker filled with ice, shake, then strain over fresh ice in the prepared rocks glass. Garnish with a lime. "When I can get my hands on a bottle of Siembra Azul, that is what I use for my marg. The agave is grown in the highlands in red clay soil and lends a nice citrusy note that connects perfectly with the simplicity of the Tommy's. Nowhere to hide in this marg; everything has got to be perfect."

Frozen JÄGERITA

BY DAVID CORDOBA FOR
28 HONGKONG STREET
IN SINGAPORE

1½ ounces Jägermeister

¾ ounce Cointreau

¾ ounce fresh lime juice

¾ ounce simple syrup (page 149)

¾ cup crushed ice

Lime wheel for garnish

Replacing the tequila in a margarita with Jägermeister may sound like a heretical dare that originated on Fraternity Row, but it's not. Illustrious bartender David Cordoba, founder of The Lovers Rum and La Forza Rum, was a global Bacardi brand ambassador when he created what has since become his signature drink. Acclaimed bartender and writer Jeffrey Morgenthaler called the amaro sour one of his guilty pleasure drinks. "I take a sip and I'm like, 'Oh my god, that's the best drink I've ever had in my life,'" he exclaimed in a Small Screen video he made about tasting the drink for the first time in 2008. Then, while working at Singapore speakeasy 28 HongKong Street in 2014, Cordoba leaned into its fun and refreshing nature by adapting it as a frozen cocktail. For his blender version, he dialed back the Cointreau and lime juice and increased the simple syrup.

Add the Jägermeister, Cointreau, lime juice, and simple syrup to a blender with the crushed ice. Blend to a smooth consistency and then pour into a double rocks glass. Garnish with a lime wheel.

Booker & Dax
BLENDER MARGARITA

BY DAVE ARNOLD FOR
BOOKER & DAX EQUIPMENT CO.
IN NEW YORK CITY

1 ounce Cointreau

¾ ounce mezcal, preferably a
robust mezcal like La Puritita

½ ounce yellow Chartreuse

½ ounce fresh lime juice

10 drops spicy bitters, preferably
Bittermens Hellfire Habanero
Shrub Bitters

5 drops 20 percent saline solution
(page 149) or a pinch of salt

4 ounces ice

When this margarita variation was served at esteemed cocktail scientist Dave Arnold's Booker & Dax bar in New York, it involved his beloved Japanese shaved ice machine and a tableside presentation. Half the cocktail was poured over the shaved ice and mezcal in the coupe. "It's not a slushy, but it's still got the crystals in it, and it's pretty cool," he says. Arnold, who also authored the James Beard Award–winning *Liquid Intelligence,* created a blender version of that drink to be enjoyed at home. For the BDx Margarita, he uses more liqueur than base spirit since the blender drink demands more sugar for body and flavor. His "secret" ingredient was yellow Chartreuse. "Whenever I had a margarita spec that wasn't quite going my way, I just added some Chartreuse to it," he explains. "It makes everything better."

Add the Cointreau, mezcal, Chartreuse, lime juice, bitters, and saline solution to a blender with the ice and bend until the ice is fully crushed, but not overblended. Pour into a coupe.

Dave's Margarita

2 ounces tequila, ¾ ounce Cointreau, ¾ ounce fresh lime juice, ¼ ounce 1:1 simple syrup (page 149), and 7 drops 20 percent saline solution (page 149).

Summer
MELON MARG

BY ANDREW BURTON FOR HORSE
INN IN LANCASTER, PENNSYLVANIA

MAKES 2 DRINKS

3 ounces blanco tequila,
preferably Tres Agaves

1 ounce Manzanilla sherry

1½ ounces fresh lime juice

10 ounces cantaloupe puree
(recipe follows)

4 cups ice

2 lime wheels for garnish

During that first summer of the pandemic in 2020, Horse Inn, a restaurant that has been in operation since Prohibition, purchased a slushy machine to create frozen cocktails to go. Head bartender Andrew Burton developed a different frozen cocktail that included cantaloupe and sherry. He quickly realized that its sweet and salty flavors worked best in the margarita format. Here, the cantaloupe's sweet and floral qualities stood in for the Cointreau, while the dry sherry's salinity not only complemented the blanco tequila's vegetal notes and minerality but subbed in beautifully for the salted rim of a traditional marg.

Add the tequila, sherry, lime juice, cantaloupe puree, and ice to a blender and blend until smooth. Pour into two 12-ounce glasses. Garnish with lime wheels.

CANTALOUPE PUREE

Cut a cantaloupe in half, scoop out the seeds, and carve out the melon's flesh, separating it from the rind. Cut the cantaloupe into chunks and place in a bowl with ½ cup of sugar and 1 teaspoon of salt until they soften. Add the softened mixture to a blender and blend until smooth. Double strain into a container, seal, and store in the refrigerator. It will keep for up to 4 days.

Andrew's Margarita

2 ounces Tres Agaves blanco tequila ("I'm partial to the crisp vegetal qualities of this tequila, and it's affordable and has no additives."), ½ ounce Cointreau, 1 ounce fresh lime juice, ½ ounce simple syrup (page 149), half rim of salt, and lime wheel garnish.

Fruity

RIFFS

Mano
A MANGO
SPICY MANGO MARGARITA

BY LYNNETTE MARRERO
IN NEW YORK CITY

1½ ounces blanco tequila

¾ ounce mango shrub (recipe follows)

¾ ounce grilled pineapple juice
(recipe follows)

½ ounce fresh lime juice

½ teaspoon hot sauce

Pinch of salt

Grilled or dehydrated
pineapple slice for garnish

When looking to create a food-friendly margarita riff for online publication Food52, co-founder of Speed Rack and highly esteemed bartender Lynnette Marrero devised this mouthwatering spicy-mango rendition, which celebrates her Puerto Rican and New Yorker roots. This marg is flavored with a homemade mango shrub, grilled pineapple juice, and a hit of hot sauce.

Add the tequila, mango shrub, pineapple juice, lime juice, hot sauce, and salt to a shaker filled with ice and shake vigorously to combine, 30 to 40 seconds. Double strain into an ice-filled rocks glass and garnish with a grilled or dehydrated pineapple slice.

MANGO SHRUB

Slice 1 ripe mango, place the slices in a jar, and add 1 cup of apple cider vinegar. Set aside. In a skillet over medium heat, toast 1 teaspoon of crushed cumin seeds and 6 crushed pink peppercorns until aromatic. Add them to the jar and screw on the lid. Store in a cool, dark place for 3 days. Taste test, checking for desired fruit flavor. Once ready, strain out the solids and gently heat the shrub in a saucepan, being careful not to boil it. Mix in 6 ounces of agave nectar, stirring until combined. Remove from the heat and let cool. The shrub will keep in the refrigerator for 2 weeks.

GRILLED PINEAPPLE JUICE

Peel, core, and slice 1 fresh pineapple. Grill the slices on a hot grill until lightly charred. Let cool then add the pineapple to a blender and blend until smooth. If it isn't juicy enough, add 1 or 2 ounces of water. Strain the juice into a bowl and stir in ½ ounce agave nectar.

Waterloo
WATERMELON MARGARITA

BY JUSTIN LAVENUE FOR
ROADHAUS MOBILE COCKTAILS
IN AUSTIN

1½ ounces mezcal,
preferably Del Maguey Vida

1 ounce fresh watermelon juice

¾ ounce fresh lime juice

½ ounce agave nectar

Watermelon half wheel slice
for garnish

Lime peel for expressing

RoadHaus Mobile Cocktails is a mobile cocktail bar for Austin's The Roosevelt Room that party hosts can hire to supercharge their event's cocktail game. Fully stocked, it offers about 75 cocktails, which include nine agave drinks, two of which are margaritas: one traditional and the other watermelon. Why watermelon, out of all the other flavored margarita options out there? According to Justin Lavenue, the fruit's flavor notes echo those of agave spirits. "Many agave spirits make it seem like you're biting into a fresh watermelon with each sip," he explains. "Thus, this pairing always seemed natural." Not to mention that the hydrating nature of watermelon harnessed in a margarita "makes it the perfect drink to sip on a hot summer day."

Add the mezcal, watermelon juice, lime juice, and agave nectar to a shaker along with three ice cubes and shake for 5 seconds. Strain over a large ice cube in a double rocks glass. Garnish with a watermelon half wheel placed inside the rim of the glass. Express lime oils from the lime peel (squeeze with the peel facing down) over the watermelon garnish.

Justin's Margarita

2 ounces blanco tequila (Tapatío, Tequila Ocho, Mijenta, or El Tesoro), 1 ounce fresh lime juice, and scant ½ ounce agave nectar. Add the ingredients to a shaker along with three ice cubes, shake for 5 seconds, then strain over a large ice cube in a frozen double rocks glass with a half rim of coarse sea salt. Express lime oils over the glass and garnish with a lime wheel.

Super Strawberry
MARGARITA

BY TREVOR EASTER AND BRITTA
CURRIE FOR THE BUTTERSCOTCH
DEN IN SACRAMENTO

1 ounce blanco tequila

½ ounce Cocchi Rosa

1 teaspoon mezcal

¾ ounce fresh lime juice

¾ ounce strawberry super sauce
(recipe follows)

Lime wheel for garnish

Trevor Easter and Britta Currie of Imbibe 75–honored bar The Butterscotch Den in Sacramento were on a mission. Their objective? To rescue the strawberry margarita from its reputation as an '80s-era sugar bomb. "The rise in popularity of sour mix and subpar strawberry syrups had unfortunately dissuaded many from ordering what could be an extraordinary beverage," Easter says. Instead of muddling strawberries into simple syrup, the duo enhanced the texture of the strawberry syrup by introducing lactic acid. Meanwhile, Cocchi Rosa, a rosé aperitif, both boosted the strawberry profile and bestowed it with nuance. "It truly is something new that feels familiar and simultaneously fun," says Easter.

Add the tequila, Cocchi Rosa, mezcal, lime juice, and strawberry super sauce to a shaker filled with ice and shake until chilled. Strain into a cactus glass over fresh ice. Garnish with a lime wheel.

STRAWBERRY SUPER SAUCE

Thaw 10½ ounces hulled frozen strawberries. Add the thawed strawberries, 1½ cups sugar, and 1 teaspoon lactic acid to a blender and blend on high for 2 minutes. ("I prefer to buy fresh strawberries and then freeze them. They really break down in the freezer. And once they're thawed, they have a more intense flavor.") The syrup will last in an airtight container in the refrigerator for 2 weeks.

Trevor's Margaritas

Option A (Buckle Up): 2 ounces blanco tequila, 1 ounce Cointreau, ¾ ounce fresh lime juice, and just a pinch of salt in the tin.

Option B (Take It Easy): 1½ ounces blanco tequila, ¾ ounce Cointreau hybrid (1:1 Cointreau and simple syrup [page 149]), ¾ ounce fresh lime juice, and just a pinch of salt in the tin.

Black Forest
MARGARITA

BY KIM HAASARUD FOR GARDEN
BAR IN PHOENIX

1½ ounces tequila alternative
spirit, preferably Clean Co
or Free Spirits

1 ounce Black Forest puree
(recipe follows)

1 ounce fresh lime juice

½ ounce simple syrup (page 149)

Dried lime wheel for garnish

According to *101 Margaritas* author Kim Haasarud, "The best margaritas are usually the simplest margaritas." When it comes to an alcohol-free margarita, though, don't go too simple or else you'll just end up with sugar and lime juice. Nonalcoholic tequilas use botanicals and spices to emulate the spirit, but they don't quite succeed in mimicking the taste of agave. So when creating a virgin margarita, Haasarud decided to go all in on flavor. "I wanted to create a robust, dark-fruit margarita that was rich, flavorful, and tasted a little more substantial than just juice and puree," she says. "This one hit the mark!"

Add the tequila alternative, Black Forest puree, lime juice, and simple syrup to a shaker filled with ice and shake until chilled. Strain over ice into a rocks glass. Garnish with a dried lime wheel.

BLACK FOREST PUREE

In a bowl, stir together 2 cups of frozen mixed berries (the mixture should include blackberries and blueberries) and 1½ cups of white sugar. Let the berries thaw in the sugar. (The sugar will bring out the juice in the berries.) Once thawed, add to a blender and pulse 2 or 3 times to break up the flesh, then add ¼ cup water and blend until the mixture is combined. Strain through a cheesecloth or tea strainer to remove the solids. Bottle and refrigerate until ready to use. The puree will keep in the refrigerator for 10 days.

Kim's Margarita

"I rarely make just one margarita at a time, so this recipe is for two." 4 ounces reposado tequila, 2 ounces 2:1 simple syrup (page 149), and 2 ounces fresh lime juice. Add all the ingredients plus four ice cubes to a blender. (This method helps aerate the cocktail and give a little ice crunch.) Blend on high until you stop hearing the crackling and breaking of the ice. Pour into two iced rocks glasses and top each one with a squeeze of lime juice from a lime wedge and drop the wedge into the glass.

Coconut
MARGARITA

BY BEAU DU BOIS FOR PUESTO
IN SAN DIEGO

2 ounces reposado tequila

¾ ounce coconut cream
(recipe follows)

½ ounce fresh lime juice

4 dashes grapefruit tincture
(recipe follows)

Sure, you can simply add coconut cream to a margarita to give it beachy vibes. But for Puesto's coconut margarita, Beau du Bois, who has worked on bar programs for Disney and Michelin-starred The Restaurant at Meadowood, brightens it up by also adding a hint of grapefruit. "In this case, the grapefruit oil extracted from the peels in the tincture helps keep the coconut flavor's feet on the ground."

Add all the ingredients to a shaker filled with ice and shake until chilled. Strain over fresh ice in a tumbler.

COCONUT CREAM

Add 6 ounces simple syrup (page 149) and 12 ounces Coco Lopez cream of coconut to a blender. Blend on high for 1 minute. The coconut cream will keep in the refrigerator for 30 days.

GRAPEFRUIT TINCTURE

Slice four grapefruits into thin wheels. Place into a sealable vessel with 750 milliliters of vodka and allow to infuse for 1 hour. Double strain the liquid, gently pressing the grapefruit wheels to extract all the juice. The tincture can be stored in the refrigerator for up to 1 year.

Beau's Margarita

2 ounces Cascahuín Blanco, ½ ounce Cointreau, 1 ounce fresh lime juice, and ½ ounce simple syrup (page 149). Add all the ingredients to a shaker filled with ice, shake, then strain over a large-format ice cube in a double rocks glass with a partial salt swath on the rim. Garnish with a lime peel.

Hang Loose
BRAH

MANGO MARGARITA

BY CHRISTINE WISEMAN FOR
BROKEN SHAKER IN LOS ANGELES

1½ ounces blanco tequila

¼ ounce Salers gentian aperitif

1 ounce mango agave syrup
(recipe follows)

¾ ounce fresh lime juice

Chamoy for rim and garnish

Tajín for rim

Mango slices for garnish

In Los Angeles, fruteros (fruit carts) on the sidewalks are a welcome sight come afternoon snack time. Their fresh-cut mango, pineapple, watermelon, and more are then spiced up with chamoy, Tajín, and salt and served in a bag. And Christine Wiseman, 2023 North America's 50 Best Bars award winner and Bar Lab Hospitality global beverage director, captures all those luscious, ripe fruit flavors and spices in her margarita. Here, she "wanted to celebrate the colors and flavors that you see in that bag, complete with the chamoy."

Dip the outside rim of half of a rocks glass in chamoy and then the Tajín, and set aside. Add the tequila, gentian, mango agave syrup, and lime juice to a shaker filled with ice and shake until chilled. Strain into the prepared glass over fresh ice. Top with mango slices and a drizzle of chamoy.

MANGO AGAVE SYRUP

Combine equal parts agave nectar and water in a saucepan over medium heat. Warm slightly, stirring until thoroughly incorporated. Remove from the heat and let cool. Once cooled, add the agave mixture and an equal amount of mango puree (frozen works perfectly) to a blender and blend until combined. The syrup will keep in the refrigerator for 7 days.

Christine's Margarita

2 ounces blanco tequila, ½ ounce Cointreau, 1 ounce fresh lime juice, and ½ ounce 1:1 agave syrup (page 149).

The Day After the
DAY OF THE DEAD

BY MATTHEW BIANCANIELLO FOR
YSABEL IN WEST HOLLYWOOD

1 ounce reposado tequila,
preferably Tequila Ocho

1 ounce mezcal, preferably Vago

¾ ounce Cynar

1 ounce blood orange juice

¾ ounce fresh lime juice

½ ounce 1:1 agave syrup
(page 149)

Marigolds for garnish

Matthew Biancaniello, author of *Eat Your Drink,* first made a name for himself in 2009 when farm-to-glass cocktails were in vogue. But he took the concept to new heights, using foraged and farmers' market–fresh produce to create mind-blowing flavor combinations. Biancaniello brought kitchen smarts to every bar program he built, from the Hollywood Roosevelt's Library Bar to Ysabel in West Hollywood.

For his The Day After the Day of the Dead Margarita, he plays up the citrus with blood orange juice and extends its bitterness with an amaro. "I usually look for layers in cocktails and notes that draw out flavors and extend finishes, and Cynar's bitterness is perfect for that," he says. He then pairs the "incredibly smooth and vivacious" Tequila Ocho with Mezcal Vago, whose fruit and cinnamon notes complement the blood orange.

Place the tequila, mezcal, Cynar, blood orange juice, lime juice, and agave syrup in a tin filled with ice and shake until chilled. Strain into a Collins glass with ice. Garnish with marigolds.

Matthew's Margarita

2 ounces Tequila Ocho Reposado, 1 ounce fresh lime juice, and ¾ ounce 1:1 agave syrup (page 149). Add all the ingredients to a shaker filled with ice, shake, then strain over a large ice cube in a double rocks glass.

Veggie
VARIATIONS

Red ZEPPELIN

RED ONION MARGARITA

BY ABIGAIL SMITH FOR BIG BAR
IN LOS ANGELES

1½ ounces reposado tequila

½ ounce Planteray Stiggins'
Fancy Pineapple rum

¾ ounce fresh lime juice

¾ ounce salted red onion syrup
(recipe follows)

½ ounce pineapple juice

Red onion skin for garnish

A red onion margarita may raise some eyebrows, but cooked and salted red onions truly make for a mouthwatering take on the classic. Bartender Abigail Smith of LA's favorite neighborhood watering hole Big Bar built this cocktail around the idea of the salted red onion syrup, combining it with her favorite ingredients (tequila, rum, and lime). "It became a complex, savory spin on something this Texan will always love—a margarita," she says. "I definitely get a lot of funny faces when I say the words 'onion margarita,' but if I had a catchphrase when bartending, it would be 'trust me.'"

Add the tequila, rum, lime juice, onion syrup, and pineapple juice to a shaker filled with ice and shake until chilled. Strain over ice into a goblet. Garnish by clipping red onion skins to the rim with a mini clothespin.

SALTED RED ONION SYRUP

Combine 2 cups water, 1 cup chopped red onions, and 1 teaspoon kosher salt in a saucepan and bring to boil. Reduce the heat and simmer for 1 hour. The onions will infuse the broth with their color. Turn off the heat and let cool for another hour. (Don't skip this part since the liquid will deepen into a beautiful pink-red as it cools.) Strain the onion pieces out of the broth and add 2 cups white cane sugar. Stir until dissolved. The syrup will last in the refrigerator for 3 weeks.

Abigail's Margarita

2 ounces Fortaleza blanco tequila, 1 ounce fresh lime juice, ½ ounce agave nectar, and a splash of olive juice. Add all the ingredients to a shaker filled with ice, shake, then dump. "I like a flavored salt, too."

Bruce
BANNER

GREEN JUICE MARGARITA

BY JULIAN COX FOR TARTINE
MANUFACTORY IN SAN FRANCISCO

1½ ounces blanco tequila,
preferably Tapatío or Fortaleza

1 teaspoon Chareau liqueur

1 ounce fresh lime juice

¾ ounce green juice (fresh or
store-bought; recipe follows)

¾ ounce 2:1 agave syrup
(page 149)

2 dashes bird's eye chile tincture
(recipe follows)

10 to 12 fresh mint leaves

Baby's breath and borage
blossoms for garnish

Back when restaurants paid more attention to their wine programs than their cocktail menus, barman Julian Cox reimagined the restaurant bar as a cocktail destination. He was trained by cocktail legend Sam Ross (inventor of the modern classic Penicillin) while working at Chef David Myers's Comme Ça in West Hollywood. Cox went on to create the James Beard–nominated bar program for the now-shuttered Rivera and the modern classic mezcal cocktail known as the Barbacoa, as well as bar programs for celebrated Los Angeles restaurants such as Bestia and Redbird. But of all the margarita-inspired cocktails he created over the years, he says this is one of his favorites. "It's a little spicy and when you drink it, you feel like you're at the spa," he says.

Add the tequila, Chareau, lime juice, green juice, agave syrup, chile tincture, and mint to a shaker filled with ice and shake to chill. Double strain into an ice-filled double rocks glass. Garnish with baby's breath and borage blossoms.

GREEN JUICE

Juice 10 tomatillos, 6 seeded and destemmed green pasilla peppers, and 2 celery stalks. Stir in a pinch of salt and 2 teaspoons ground coriander. The juice will keep in the refrigerator for 1 week.

BIRD'S EYE CHILE TINCTURE

Add 3 tablespoons kosher salt and ⅓ cup chopped fresh bird's eye chile to 2 cups plus 2 tablespoons high-proof (151-proof) vodka. Allow to infuse for 30 to 45 minutes, tasting every 5 minutes to check the spice level. Once it's as spicy as you prefer, strain out the chiles. The tincture will keep in the refrigerator for 4 weeks.

Julian's Margarita

2 ounces blanco tequila (such as Tequila Ocho), ¼ ounce Combier, 1 ounce fresh lime juice, and ½ ounce raw agave nectar. Make a half rim of salt on your chilled double rocks glass. Add all the ingredients to a shaker filled with ice. Zest a lime and lemon over the top of the shaker, which "will significantly brighten your drink, and it becomes even more crushable." Vigorously shake, then double strain over ice or a king cube. Garnish with a lime wedge.

PODRACER

PEA SOTOL MARGARITA

BY STUART WEAVER FOR
LADY JANE IN DENVER

1½ ounces English pea–infused
sotol (recipe follows)

¾ ounce mint syrup
(recipe follows)

¾ ounce fresh lime juice

Fresh mint sprigs for garnish

As an ode to spring, Stuart Weaver, general manager of Lady Jane in Denver, wanted a margarita that showcased his favorite seasonal produce. In creating this novel version, he traded out the tequila for sotol. "Sotol is made from the Desert Spoon plant, which is in the asparagus family," he says. "And what screams 'spring' more than asparagus, peas, and mint?!" He prefers the La Higuera Cedrosanum sotol for its bright vegetal notes. For those who can't find that bottle, Weaver recommends looking for a sotol that is "particularly vegetal and earthy while not being a smoke bomb."

Add the infused sotol, mint syrup, and lime juice to a shaker filled with ice and shake to chill. Double strain into a coupe. Garnish by pinning a mint bouquet to the rim.

ENGLISH PEA–INFUSED SOTOL

Add 1 cup pea shoots and ¾ cup English peas (washed, opened, and separated shells and peas) to a 750-milliliter bottle of sotol. Let the mixture sit at room temperature for 24 hours. Strain into a bottle. The infused sotol will keep in the refrigerator for 3 months.

MINT SYRUP

Combine 1 cup water and 1 cup sugar in a saucepan. Cook and stir over medium heat until the sugar is dissolved. Remove from the heat and add 2 cups firmly packed mint leaves while the mixture is still warm. Let the mixture steep at room temperature for 30 minutes. Strain and store in the refrigerator for up to 1 month.

Stuart's Margarita

2 ounces Fortaleza blanco tequila, ¾ ounce Cointreau, ¾ ounce fresh lime juice, and ¼ ounce simple syrup (page 149) or agave nectar. Add all the ingredients to a shaker filled with ice, shake, then double strain over Hoshizaki ice in a half-salt-rimmed rocks glass. Garnish with a lime wedge.

Low ALTITUDE

LOW-PROOF MARGARITA

BY NATASHA DAVID
IN NEW YORK CITY

1½ ounces Pineau des Charentes

½ ounce blanco tequila

½ ounce génépy

¾ ounce fresh lime juice

½ ounce vanilla syrup
(recipe follows)

1 dash celery bitters

Lime wheel for garnish

Natasha David has been celebrated many times over as both a bartender (2015 Star Chefs Rising Star and *Imbibe* magazine's 2020 Bartender of the Year) and owner of award-winning New York City bar Nitecap, which shuttered in 2020. But as someone who isn't big on getting tipsy, she ended up writing about low- and no-alcohol cocktails for her book *Drink Lightly* during the period when she was shutting down her bar. For her low-proof margarita, David developed a way to stretch a half-ounce of tequila by enhancing its bright vegetal notes with génépy (an herbal liqueur) and celery bitters. "To play with the richness of the Pineau des Charentes [a French aperitif made of cognac and grape juice], I chose vanilla, which also pairs beautifully with the celery and herbal notes," she explains. "The result is a luscious yet fresh spin on a margarita."

Add the Pineau des Charentes, tequila, génépy, lime juice, vanilla syrup, and celery bitters to a shaker filled with ice and shake until chilled. Strain into a double rocks glass over ice. Garnish with a lime wheel.

VANILLA SYRUP

Add 2 cups 1:1 simple syrup (page 149), 1 teaspoon Tahitian vanilla extract, ¾ teaspoon lactic acid, and a pinch of kosher salt to a medium bowl. Whisk to combine until the lactic acid and salt are dissolved. The syrup will keep in the refrigerator for up to 4 weeks.

Natasha's Margarita

2 ounces El Tesoro Platinum, 1 ounce Cointreau, and ¾ ounce fresh lime juice. Generously rim a double rocks glass with salt (2 parts kosher to 1 part Maldon smoked salt) and set aside (see page 23). Add all the ingredients to a shaker filled with ice, shake, then strain into the prepared glass with ice. Garnish with a lime wedge.

Spa Day
MARGARITA

BY CHRIS BOSTICK FOR
HALF STEP BAR IN AUSTIN

2 ounces blanco tequila,
preferably Tequila Ocho

1 ounce fresh lime juice

¾ ounce dry curaçao,
preferably Pierre Ferrand

¼ ounce 1:1 simple syrup
(page 149)

2 (¼-inch) slices English cucumber,
plus more for garnish

2 seedless red grapes,
plus more for garnish

This margarita wasn't created to be enjoyed after a sauna. It was actually inspired by another cocktail. Before returning to Austin to open his bar, Half Step, Chris Bostick had managed The Varnish in Los Angeles when it was named 2012 Best American Cocktail Bar at Tales of the Cocktail. There, he had created a cocktail with Jamaican rum and grapes. But here he adds cucumber. "I love the combo of grapes and cucumbers," he explains. "[It] creates a very fresh, cooling, and lively margarita. Perfect for the Texas heat and patio drinking."

Add the cucumber slices, grapes, lime juice, curaçao, and simple syrup to a shaker and muddle the cucumber slices and grapes. Add the tequila and fill the shaker with ice and shake until chilled. Strain over fresh ice in a double rocks glass and garnish with a grape speared onto a cucumber slice.

Chris's Margarita

2 ounces Tequila Ocho Plata, ¾ ounce Mathilde XO orange liqueur, 1 ounce fresh lime juice, and ¼ ounce simple syrup (page 149). Add all the ingredients to a shaker filled with ice, shake, then strain over fresh ice.

Margarita
VERDE

BY STACEY SWENSON
IN NEW YORK CITY

1¾ ounces blanco tequila,
preferably El Tesoro

½ ounce Salers gentian aperitif

¾ ounce garden cordial
(recipe follows)

¾ ounce fresh lime juice

2 dashes 20 percent saline
solution (page 149)

2 dashes Tabasco green
jalapeño sauce

Lime wheel and parsley sprig
for garnish

In 2018, when Stacey Swenson was the head bartender at Dante, which was named World's Best Bar and Best American Restaurant Bar at the 2019 Spirited Awards, she took part in the "bartender residency" at online publication *Punch*, which spotlighted up-and-coming bartenders. For her month-long takeover, Swenson wanted to create a verdant margarita-inspired cocktail that not only showcased the grassiness of blanco tequila but also looked exactly like how it tasted: "very green in every way." She skipped the plain agave syrup, and in its place blended up a cordial made with freshly juiced green vegetables and agave nectar. You'll need a juicer for making the juices in the garden cordial.

Add the tequila, Salers, garden cordial, lime juice, saline solution, and green Tabasco to a shaker filled with ice and shake until chilled. Strain over ice into a rocks glass. Garnish with a lime wheel and parsley sprig.

GARDEN CORDIAL

Add 1 cup of fresh green bell pepper juice, 1 cup of whole snap peas, a handful of parsley, 1 cup of fresh celery juice, 2 cups of agave nectar, and 1 cup of water to a Vitamix or blender. Blend until smooth and double strain. The cordial will keep in the refrigerator for 7 days.

Stacey's Margarita

2 ounces tequila or mezcal, ½ ounce orange curaçao, 1 ounce fresh lime juice, and ½ ounce agave syrup (page 149). Add all the ingredients to a shaker filled with ice, shake, then strain over fresh ice in a glass with a half-rim of salt. Garnish with a lime wheel.

Spicy
SELECTIONS

Margarita
TOREADA

SERRANO CHILE SPICY MARGARITA

BY BRICIA LOPEZ IN LOS ANGELES

MAKES 8 DRINKS

1 small serrano chile

8 ounces blanco tequila

8 ounces reposado tequila

8 ounces fresh lime juice

8 ounces simple syrup (page 149)

2 cups ice

Lime wedges for rim

Tajín for rim

For her second book, *Asada: The Art of Mexican-Style Grilling* (co-written with Javier Cabral), which focuses on grilled food and good times, Bricia Lopez, co-owner of Guelaguetza in Los Angeles, wanted to add a roasted element to the spicy margarita. She threw a serrano chile on the grill and then muddled it into the marg. She discovered that doing so created "that beautiful roasted flavor without having to use mezcal." As for the use of two different tequilas, Lopez says, "You don't really need to buy two. Blancos tend to be more affordable, so you can definitely get away with just using blanco. If it's all blanco, it's going to be just as good. It's just very clean, very sharp, and refreshing."

Rim eight rocks glasses with Tajín and set aside (see page 23). Roast the chile: If using a grill, place the chile over the fire, charring it all over. Alternately, on the stovetop, char the chile in a cast-iron pan over medium heat. Stem, seed, and slice the chile. Then drop it into a pitcher and muddle it. Add the tequilas, lime juice, simple syrup, and ice then stir to combine. To serve, add fresh ice and 4 ounces of the cocktail to each glass.

Bricia's Margarita

"I'm a Tommy's kind of gal. Just fresh lime, agave, and blanco. I don't like triple sec. I just want those three things and a half-salted rim and half Tajín or chamoy to add that other element."

EL MORADO

SPICY BLACK CURRANT MARGARITA

BY GABY MLYNARCZYK FOR
BIRCH IN LOS ANGELES

1½ ounces jalapeño-infused
tequila (or Manzanilla sherry;
recipe follows)

1 ounce crème de cassis,
preferably Massenez

1 ounce fresh lime juice

½ ounce simple syrup (page 149)

Pinch of sea salt

1 to 3 dashes Scrappy's Firewater
Habanero Tincture (optional)

Lime wheel for garnish

Lauded bartender and *Drink Up and Glow* author Gaby Mlynarczyk's long career has been transforming restaurants, such as those by celebrated chefs Michael Voltaggio and Brendan Collins, into destination drink spots for unique culinary-inspired cocktails. For what ended up being her favorite margarita-inspired creation, she combines a spicy currant jelly and Trader Vic's El Diablo highball. The result is a bright and vegetal marg with ripe, dark fruitiness and sea salt enhancing the flavors. For a sessionable version, try her low-proof option made with jalapeño-infused sherry. "The low ABV has a little more nuttiness and salinity because of the Manzanilla sherry," she says. "It's also much more crushable."

Add the infused tequila, crème de cassis, lime juice, simple syrup, sea salt, and tincture (if using) to a shaker with 4 or 5 Kold-Draft ice cubes and shake hard for 5 seconds. Strain into a chilled ice-filled rocks glass. Garnish with a lime wheel.

JALAPEÑO-INFUSED TEQUILA (OR MANZANILLA SHERRY)

Add 1 chopped jalapeño to a 375-milliliter bottle of silver tequila or Manzanilla sherry. Allow to infuse for at least 24 hours then strain into a bottle. The infused tequila can be stored in the refrigerator for up to 3 months.

Gaby's Margarita

1½ ounces Yuu Baal mezcal, ¾ ounce Pierre Ferrand dry curaçao, 1 ounce fresh lime juice, 1 bar spoon of simple syrup (page 149), a pinch of Maldon smoked sea salt, and a dash of Scrappy's Firewater Habanero Tincture to give it a bit of heat.

Picante
AMANTE

SPICY PRICKLY PEAR MARGARITA

BY JOHN HARDIN FOR DUSK BAR
IN SANTA BARBARA

1½ ounces blanco tequila,
preferably Don Fulano or Mijenta

½ ounce mezcal, preferably Bozal
Ensamble or Amarás Verde

1 ounce fresh lime juice

¾ ounce prickly pear syrup,
preferably Liquid Alchemist
or Real

3 dashes spicy tincture (recipe
follows or Scrappy's Firewater
Habanero Tincture)

Lime wedge for rim and garnish

Pink peppercorn salt for rim
(recipe follows)

Santa Barbara, California, known as the American Riviera, features many a margarita. There's a hotel bar on State Street that boasts some of the best riffs around. When John Hardin was the beverage director of the Drift Hotel's Dusk Bar, he built an impressively extensive selection of agave spirits and created house-made syrups, liqueurs, and tinctures to better control the consistency of the cocktails. His standout was this magenta-vibrant spicy margarita variation inspired by his childhood in Coachella Valley, where the prickly pear is the local fruit. With the classic margarita as the vehicle, Hardin created what he says "is everything a cocktail enthusiast could ask for in a margarita— a tart, prickly pear–sweetened margarita, with the addition of a bit of mezcal, habanero spice, all combined with the unique savoriness of pink peppercorn salt on the rim." At the bar, Hardin made his own prickly pear syrup but to keep things simple he offers store-bought options here.

Rim a rocks glass with pink peppercorn salt and set aside (see page 23). Add the tequila, mezcal, lime juice, prickly pear cordial, and spicy tincture to a shaker filled with ice and shake to chill. Strain into the prepared glass over fresh ice. Garnish with a lime wedge.

SPICY TINCTURE

Add 6 chopped habaneros to 1 cup of vodka. Allow the mixture to sit for at least 10 days and then strain out the habaneros. Make sure to taste it often until it reaches your desired spiciness. This tincture will keep indefinitely.

PINK PEPPERCORN SALT

Combine equal parts of kosher salt and pink peppercorns in a blender. Blend until thoroughly mixed.

Christmas
MARGARITA

HATCH GREEN CHILE MARGARITA

BY NATALIE BOVIS IN SANTA FE

1½ ounces reposado tequila

½ ounce Ancho Reyes
ancho chile liqueur

½ ounce orange liqueur

1 tablespoon seeded, diced fresh
Hatch green chile (or jalapeño)

½ to ¾ ounce fresh lime juice

Lime wedge for rim

Christmas spice mix for rim
(recipe follows)

Natalie Bovis started blogging about cocktails in 2006 in Los Angeles as *The Liquid Muse*. Fast-forward to now, and she's the author of several cocktail books, including *Edible Cocktails;* the co-founder of OM Chocolate Liqueur; and a culinary event producer. Bovis actually created this spicy, vegetal margarita variation for her 2016 New Mexico Cocktails & Culture event. However, it is inspired not by colored holiday lights but rather the style of Santa Fe dishes called "Christmas" for using both red and green chiles. They're the only region in the Southwest to combine both types of chiles. And in her ode to New Mexico, she highlights its famous Hatch green chile in the marg, muddling in the fresh chile, amping up its flavor with chile liqueur, and rimming the glass with red and green chile powder.

Rim a rocks glass with Christmas spice mix and set aside (see page 23). Add the chile and lime juice to a cocktail shaker, muddle together, then add the tequila and both liqueurs. Fill the shaker with ice and shake until chilled. Gently strain into the rimmed glass.

CHRISTMAS SPICE MIX

Combine equal parts of sugar, kosher salt, and ground red and green chile powder.

Natalie's Margarita

1½ ounces blanco tequila, ¾ ounce orange liqueur, ¾ ounce mix of equal parts lemon and lime juice, splash grapefruit juice ("I love this and often add it when I'm making a drink for myself at home."), and 1 bar spoon agave nectar. Rim a rocks or margarita glass with a sugar and pink sea salt mix, fill the glass with ice, set aside. Add all the ingredients to a shaker filled with ice, shake, then strain into the glass.

MALCRIADA

BY CHRISTIAN SUZUKI-ORELLANA
FOR WILDHAWK IN SAN FRANCISCO

1½ ounces mezcal

¾ ounce basil eau de vie,
preferably St. George
Aqua Perfecta

½ ounce genever

¼ ounce lychee liqueur,
preferably Giffard

½ ounce fresh lime juice

¼ ounce simple syrup (page 149)

2 dashes togarashi tincture
(recipe follows)

Thai basil leaf for garnish

Imbibe 75 honoree and Netflix's *Drink Masters* alum Christian "Suzu" Suzuki-Orellana loves celebrating his Japanese heritage through his cocktails. His margarita-inspired mezcal cocktail brings together lychee, basil, and the earthy spiciness of togarashi. Since Suzu is spice shy, he appreciates a more subtle heat in cocktails. "In this case, the aromatics are coming from the lychee and basil, and the heat is from the togarashi," he explains. "This cocktail is a demure introduction to spicy cocktails."

Add the mezcal, basil eau de vie, genever, lychee liqueur, lime juice, simple syrup, and tincture to a shaker filled with ice and shake until chilled. Double strain into a rocks glass over ice. Garnish with a Thai basil leaf.

TOGARASHI TINCTURE

Add 1 (0.63-ounce) bottle of togarashi to 8 ounces high-proof vodka. Allow to infuse for 24 hours and strain into a bottle. The tincture will keep for at least 2 months.

Christian's Margarita

2 ounces El Pintor blanco tequila, 1 ounce fresh lime juice, and ½ ounce agave nectar. "I don't need salt for my rim, but I do shake it with an orange peel. El Pintor is a little bit of a splurge for a margarita, but it's what I use if I'm making it for myself or friends at home."

SONÁMBULA

BY IVY MIX FOR FORT DEFIANCE
IN BROOKLYN

2 ounces jalapeño-infused blanco
tequila (recipe follows)

1 ounce fresh lemon juice

¾ ounce chamomile tea syrup
(2:1 sugar to strong
chamomile tea)

2 dashes mole bitters,
preferably Bittermens

2 dashes Peychaud's bitters

Lemon wheel for garnish

Ivy Mix—2015 Tales of the Cocktail Best American Bartender and author of *Spirits of Latin America*—has plenty of margarita riffs. But this one is special as it's the first cocktail she's ever put on a menu. Even now, it continues to be a staple at her James Beard–nominated bar Leyenda in Brooklyn. The spicy sour, whose name means "sleepwalker" in Spanish, features a jalapeño tequila to fire you up and is sweetened with a syrup infused with a favorite bedtime tea.

Add the tequila, lemon juice, tea syrup, and bitters to a shaker and shake for about 8 seconds. Strain into a coupe. Garnish with a lemon wheel.

JALAPEÑO-INFUSED BLANCO TEQUILA

Slice off the ends of one or two jalapeños and discard. Then chop up the rest of the peppers and drop them into a 750-milliliter bottle of tequila (preferably Arette). "I generally use *just* the seeds of one or two jalapeños (no pepper flesh) or one or two chopped-up peppers *with* seeds," says Mix. Allow to infuse for 10 to 20 minutes. Taste after 10 minutes to check for preferred spice level. If you want it spicier, leave the peppers in longer. If you find it too spicy, simply add more tequila. Strain into a bottle.

Ivy's Margarita

1½ ounces tequila, ¾ ounce Cointreau, ¾ ounce fresh lime juice, and ¼ ounce simple syrup (page 149).

Maison MARGARITA DE JAMAICA

BY WILLIAM ELLIOTT FOR MAISON
PREMIERE IN BROOKLYN

¾ ounce hibiscus-infused
overproof tequila (recipe follows)

½ ounce reposado tequila

½ ounce Combier

¼ ounce Empirical Spirits Ayuuk

¼ ounce raicilla, preferably
La Venenosa Raicilla Sierra
de Jalisco Black Label

¼ ounce lime cordial
(recipe follows)

3 dashes orange bitters,
preferably Regans'

Lime peel for expressing

Hibiscus blossom for garnish

Even though world-renowned New York bar Maison Premiere specializes in serving oysters and absinthe, bar director William Elliott says that the classic margarita is a top request. And it isn't even on the menu. "I personally love a margarita, and I've always wanted to bring more agave drinks to Maison Premiere," he says. Since the bar has a specific focus in terms of era and point of view, he wanted to create a margarita that felt right in the space. The hibiscus makes for a more impactful visual while still being in line with Maison's Victorian-era style. The drink gets its heat from the pasilla chile distillate called Ayuuk, which makes it "like a spicy margarita without actually being spicy or having to call it that, which is the last thing that I would do at Maison," he explains. Now it's one of the top five most popular cocktails at the bar.

Add the tequilas, Combier, Ayuuk, raicilla, lime cordial, and bitters to a shaker filled with ice and shake until chilled. Double strain into a coupe. Express with the lime peel and garnish with a hibiscus blossom.

HIBISCUS-INFUSED OVERPROOF TEQUILA

Add ¼ cup of dried hibiscus to a 750-milliliter bottle of tequila (preferably El Luchador 110-proof blanco) and allow to infuse for 24 hours. Strain. The tequila will keep indefinitely.

LIME CORDIAL

Add the zest of 3 limes and 1 cup of sugar to a container with a lid. Cover and leave for up to 24 hours at room temperature. Agitate every now and then. Add 1 cup of fresh lime juice and ½ ounce of vodka. Stir thoroughly until the sugar is completely dissolved. Strain through a fine-mesh strainer. The cordial will keep in the refrigerator for 1 month.

Margarita
AL PASTOR

BY BENJAMIN PADRÓN
FOR LICORERÍA LIMANTOUR
IN MEXICO CITY

1¾ ounces blanco tequila

¾ ounce Cointreau

1½ ounces taco mix syrup
(recipe follows)

¾ ounce fresh lime juice

Lime wedge and cilantro salt for
rim (recipe follows)

Pineapple wedge for garnish

Although the margarita is said to have originated in Mexico, the cocktail itself isn't all that popular in the country—contrary to what Americans believe. Locals prefer easy-to-make Palomas. (Throw tequila and lime juice into an ice-filled glass, top with grapefruit soda. Done.) Thirsty tourists can find margaritas at resorts. But when Licorería Limantour opened in Mexico City with an eye toward craft cocktails, co-founder Benjamin Padrón decided to put this margarita on the menu to accommodate the tourists who comprised half of the bar's patrons. The bar has been a regular on the World's 50 Best Bars list since 2014. The cocktail, which is spiced with a homemade taco mix, was inspired by the most popular taco in Mexico City.

Rim a rocks glass with cilantro salt and set aside (see page 23). Add the tequila, Cointreau, taco mix syrup, and lime juice to a shaker filled with ice and shake until chilled. Strain over fresh ice into the glass. Garnish with a pineapple wedge.

TACO MIX SYRUP

Begin by making a serrano chile–infused agave syrup. Add 3 tablespoons chopped serrano chile and 7 tablespoons water in a small pot over low heat. Allow to infuse for 10 minutes. Remove from the heat and let cool. Double strain and then mix the infused water with 1⅓ cups agave syrup (page 149). Store in a bottle. (The chile-infused agave syrup will keep in the refrigerator for 3 days.) To make the taco mix syrup, add 1½ cups plus 1 tablespoon pineapple juice, ½ cup serrano chile–infused agave syrup, 5 tablespoons water, 1 cup firmly packed cilantro, ¾ cup firmly packed mint, and ¾ cup firmly packed basil to a blender and blend until smooth. Double strain into a bottle. The taco mix syrup will keep in the refrigerator for 3 days.

CILANTRO SALT

Combine 10 parts sea salt to 9 parts dried cilantro.

Georgia O'KEEFFE

BY JEN LEN FOR JONATHAN CLUB
IN LOS ANGELES

1½ ounces blanco tequila

½ ounce serrano chile–infused
mezcal (recipe follows)

¾ ounce fresh lime juice

¾ ounce hibiscus-infused honey
(recipe follows)

1 (1-inch) cube fresh pineapple
or ¼ ounce fresh pineapple juice

Edible pansy for garnish

In 2013, when drink creator Jen Len was running the bar program at private social club Jonathan Club in downtown Los Angeles, she wanted to create a tropical cocktail with hibiscus and pineapple. Recognizing that the margarita template was the best way to showcase the agave spirit, and one that "always sells," she put together this vibrant pink drink. Made with serrano-infused mezcal, hibiscus honey, and pineapple, "it's an undeniably great drink and a stunning color," she says. "And as soon as I put an edible pansy on it, the name naturally came forward."

If using fresh pineapple, add the cube to a shaker and muddle. Follow with the tequila, chile-infused mezcal, lime juice, honey, and pineapple juice (if fresh pineapple cube was not added) along with ice and shake until chilled. Strain over a large ice cube in a double rocks glass. Garnish with an edible pansy.

SERRANO CHILE–INFUSED MEZCAL

Add 1 chopped serrano chile (about dime-size slices) to a 750-milliliter bottle of mezcal and allow to infuse for 2 to 4 hours, checking the spice level regularly. The spice should be present but not overwhelming. Strain through a fine-mesh strainer to remove the seeds and chile. "The Historias y Memorias, Agave de Cortes, and Nuestra Soledad Santiago Matatlán mezcals are all well-made, not oversmoked, and an appropriate ABV for cocktails," says Len.

HIBISCUS-INFUSED HONEY

In a small pot, combine ¾ cup water and 2 tablespoons dried hibiscus, stirring over low heat. Bring to a boil and boil for 2 minutes. Strain the liquid into a measuring cup. Add an equal part (by volume) of honey. Whisk until fully incorporated and let cool. The honey will keep in the refrigerator for 1 month.

28 Guava Spicy
MARGARITA

BY THE TEAM AT 28 HONGKONG
STREET IN SINGAPORE

1⅓ ounces reposado tequila

2 teaspoons mezcal joven

1 ounce guava agave syrup
(recipe follows)

½ ounce fresh lime juice

3 dashes of Scrappy's Firewater
Habanero Tincture

2 dashes of 10 percent saline
solution (page 149)

Lime wedge for rim and garnish

Tajín and salted plum powder
(1:1) for rim

Since the Tommy's Margarita is popular among local and international customers at Singapore's 28 HongKong Street, one of the best bars in Asia, the bar team wanted to create their own Southeast Asian variation. "We decided to implement a little bit of local tropical flavor from pink guava," explains 28HKS general manager Lukas Kaufmann, "as well as add a little bit of 'heat,' which is very popular and widely used in this part of the world, in the form of Scrappy's Firewater."

Rim a double rocks glass with Tajín and salted plum powder and set in the freezer (see page 23). Add the tequila, mezcal, guava agave syrup, lime juice, tincture, and saline solution to a shaker filled with ice and shake until chilled. Double strain over ice in the chilled glass. Garnish with a lime wedge.

GUAVA AGAVE SYRUP

Wash and trim both ends of 3 to 4 ripe pink guavas and remove any brown parts. Chop the guavas, place in a blender, and blend briefly. (Store-bought organic pink guava puree will work, too.) Strain the puree through a fine-mesh strainer. Combine 3 parts guava puree with 1 part organic agave nectar. The syrup will keep in the refrigerator for 7 days.

Lukas's Margarita

Add 1 ounce blanco tequila, ½ ounce Cointreau, ⅓ ounce mezcal reposado, 1 ounce fresh lime juice, and ⅓ ounce organic agave nectar to a shaker filled with ice and shake until chilled. Strain over ice. Garnish with a Tajín-seasoned pineapple slice.

Crafty

TAKES

Vast Acid
MARGARITA

BY CHOCKIE TOM IN LONDON

1½ ounces blanco tequila,
preferably G4

¾ ounce Cointreau

1 ounce Sūpāsawā

¾ ounce nori syrup
(recipe follows)

½ ounce tepache

Lime wedge and seaweed salt
(recipe follows) for rim

As an acclaimed bartender and writer whose mission it is to champion Indigenous culture, it makes sense that Chockie Tom's margarita does just that. "I wanted to take a more sustainable approach to it, while reflecting on some of the origins of pre-Columbian ancestral fermented beverages like tepache," she explains. "I think this drink not only embraces the traditional sour flavor profile, but also enhances it with coastal ingredients." Tom usually makes her own tepache (a fermented cold beverage made from pineapple peels and brown sugar or piloncillo) since she goes through so many pineapples for her pop-up cocktail events. But those who aren't DIYers have her blessing to sub in a quality store-bought tepache.

Rim a highball glass with seaweed salt and set aside (see page 23). Add the tequila, Cointreau, Sūpāsawā, and nori syrup to a shaker filled with ice and shake until chilled. Strain over ice into the prepared glass. Top with tepache.

SEAWEED SALT

Combine ¼ cup dried seaweed with 2 tablespoons flaky sea salt. The salt will keep for up to 2 months.

NORI SYRUP

Add ½ cup granulated sugar and ½ cup water to a small saucepan over medium heat and bring to a boil, stirring to dissolve the sugar. Remove the pan from the heat. Cut half a nori sheet into 1-inch pieces and add to the syrup. Steep for about 3 hours, or until the desired flavor is achieved. Make sure to taste the syrup hourly, checking for intensity. Double strain into a sealable glass bottle and discard the solids or dehydrate them to use as garnish. The syrup will keep for about 1 month.

Mano
DE CHANGO

BY KIM STODEL FOR PROVIDENCE
IN LOS ANGELES

1½ ounces blanco tequila,
preferably Angelisco

½ ounce dry curaçao, preferably
Pierre Ferrand

1 ounce fresh grapefruit juice

½ ounce fresh lime juice

¾ ounce guava syrup
(recipe follows)

Fresh guava wedge or slice
for garnish

This crushable margarita riff marked the beginning of celebrated Los Angeles beverage director Kim Stodel's journey into sustainable cocktails where he minimized waste by reusing any byproducts of the process. It also marked his first successful attempt at making fruit leather. "It was a big 'aha!' moment and would become the basis for many pulp-into-leather garnishes to follow," he says. However, since not many people have a dehydrator at home, fresh guava can serve as the garnish here instead of the fruit leather. In this cocktail, lime and grapefruit juices are combined to soften the acid and balance the dry curaçao and guava syrup with a dry bitterness. You have the option to sweeten each sip by taking a bite out of the fresh fruit.

Add the tequila, curaçao, grapefruit juice, lime juice, and guava syrup to a cocktail shaker filled with ice and shake until chilled. Double strain into a martini glass. Garnish with guava on a pick or a guava slice on top of the drink.

GUAVA SYRUP

Peel and slice 7 ounces of guava (about 5 guavas). Place in a glass bowl with 1 cup of sugar and ¼ cup plus 1 tablespoon of water then mix until the sugar is dissolved. Cover and refrigerate the mixture for 12 to 24 hours. Stir a bit to help the sugar dissolve. (Ideally, this can be done a day in advance and left overnight in the refrigerator.) Strain the syrup from the fruit pulp. This makes 1 cup of syrup, which will keep in the refrigerator for about 1 week.

Kim's Margarita

2 ounces Tapatío blanco tequila, ¾ ounce fresh lime juice, and ½ ounce 2:1 agave syrup (page 149). Add all the ingredients to a shaker filled with ice and shake until chilled. Strain over an ice-filled rocks glass with a salt rim.

BLT
MARGARITA

RUBY RED GRAPEFRUIT AND BAY LEAF MARGARITA

BY SARAH CROWL FOR BETTER
LUCK TOMORROW IN HOUSTON

2 ounces blanco tequila,
preferably El Tesoro

1 ounce fresh lime juice

½ ounce Ruby Red and bay leaf
curaçao (recipe follows)

½ ounce agave syrup (page 149)

Lime wedge and bay leaf salt
(recipe follows) for rim

Grapefruit wheel, bay leaf,
half Key lime for garnish

While working as the bar director at Bobby Heugel and Justin Yu's Houston bar and restaurant, Sarah Crowl created this margarita inspired by Texas. "The grapefruit itself is close to home for a lot of Texans. We love our Texas Ruby Reds!" she enthuses. Homemade Ruby Red and bay curaçao replaces the orange liqueur, elevating the traditional citrus element of the cocktail, while the grapefruit zest's subtle floral notes complement the green herbal aspects of the tequila, according to Crowl. The minty and peppery aromas of the bay laurel leaves contrast with the salt and lime.

Rim a Collins glass with bay leaf salt and set aside (see page 23). Add the tequila, lime juice, Ruby Red and bay leaf curaçao, and agave syrup to a shaker filled with ice and shake until chilled. Dump into the prepared glass. Garnish with a grapefruit wheel, fresh bay leaf, and half a Key lime.

RUBY RED AND BAY LEAF CURAÇAO

Peel 1 or 2 (depending on juiciness) medium Ruby Red grapefruits and set aside peel. Juice the grapefruits and 2 limes. Add ½ cup of the grapefruit juice, ¼ cup of the lime juice, 1¼ cups water, and ¼ cup lightly packed fresh bay leaves (or ⅛ cup dried) to a saucepan over medium-high heat. Express the reserved grapefruit peel over the mixture to expose the citrus oils and then add the peel to the mixture. Bring the mixture to a boil, then reduce the heat to medium and add 1 cup sugar. Cook, stirring, until the sugar has dissolved. Remove from the heat and let cool. Refrigerate for 24 hours. Strain through a fine-mesh strainer into a bottle. To calculate the tequila needed to make the syrup into a cordial, the volume of the tequila should be equivalent to half of the volume

of the strained syrup. Whisk to incorporate. The curaçao will keep for a few months when stored in an airtight container in the refrigerator.

BAY LEAF SALT

Add 1 cup kosher salt and 12 fresh bay leaves to a food processor and pulse to achieve desired color and aroma. Discard any unprocessed bay leaves; small flecks of bay leaves will be present. Store in an airtight container.

Sarah's Margarita

2 ounces blanco tequila, 1 ounce fresh lime juice, and ¾ ounce light agave syrup (page 149) in a salt-rimmed glass with a lime wedge.

Southbound
SUAREZ

BY JEFFREY MORGENTHALER
AND BENJAMIN AMBERG FOR
CLYDE COMMON IN PORTLAND

1½ ounces reposado tequila

1½ ounces horchata
(recipe follows)

½ ounce agave syrup (page 149)

½ ounce lime juice

1 teaspoon Becherovka

Lime wedge for garnish

While working on a horchata cocktail at the now-closed Clyde Common in Portland with then lead bartender Benjamin Amberg, Jeffrey Morgenthaler couldn't come up with a recipe that would work with the sweet rice milk. Not even horchata White Russian variations were cutting it. Just when the duo was about to call it quits, they decided to add it to a margarita riff instead. Even in a citrusy drink, they knew the rice milk wouldn't curdle. "It was such a wild idea to use sweet, creamy rice milk drink in a sour/margarita formula, but it's just insane enough to work," says Morgenthaler, who is the author of *The Bar Book* and co-owner of Pacific Standard in Portland, in addition to being an award-winning bartender. The added Becherovka, an herbal bitters, bridges together the tequila and spiced horchata.

Add the tequila, horchata, agave syrup, lime juice, and Becherovka to a shaker filled with ice and shake until chilled. Strain into a rocks glass over fresh ice. Garnish with a lime wedge.

HORCHATA

Combine 1 cup California long-grain rice, 3 cups hot water, one 3-inch-long Ceylon soft cinnamon stick (broken into pieces), and ½ cup baker's (ultrafine) sugar in a mixing bowl and stir until the sugar is dissolved. Cover the bowl and let it rest in the refrigerator for up to 24 hours. Pour the mixture into a blender and blend on high speed until the rice is fine, 1 to 2 minutes. Strain through a nut milk bag into a bowl. The horchata will keep in the refrigerator for 4 days.

Jeffrey's Margarita

1½ ounces blanco tequila, ¾ ounce Cointreau, ¾ ounce fresh lime juice, and 1 teaspoon 2:1 agave syrup (page 149). Combine all the ingredients in a shaker filled with ice, shake, then strain over ice into a chilled rocks glass. Garnish with a lime wedge.

Hocus
POCUS

BY DANIELLE CROUCH AND
ALLAN KATZ FOR JAMMYLAND
IN LAS VEGAS

2 ounces blanco tequila

¾ ounce fresh lime juice

¾ ounce rosé cordial
(recipe follows)

2 dashes lavender bitters,
preferably Cocktail Punk

2 (1¼-inch) cubes watermelon
or equivalent (same size as a
Kold-Draft cube)

Lime wheel for garnish

After years of schooling from cocktail legends such as Dale DeGroff, Julie Reiner, and Tony Abou-Ganim, Danielle Crouch and Allan Katz exhibit a lightheartedness and approachable cocktail geekiness in their drink creations. Their margarita variation, which is their most popular cocktail at their Jamaican-inspired bar and restaurant Jammyland in Las Vegas's Arts District, is based on one of their favorite New York cocktails. The Vamos a la Playa is an aged rum and watermelon cocktail by former Clover Club bartender Katie Stipe. But instead of the coriander cordial Stipe uses in the Vamos, Crouch and Katz created a cordial with a bone-dry rosé, contributing a minerality to the drink while also sweetening it.

Add the tequila, lime juice, rosé cordial, lavender bitters, and watermelon cubes to a shaker filled with ice and shake until chilled. Double strain into a coupe. Garnish with a lime wheel.

ROSÉ CORDIAL

Measure equal parts by weight rosé wine and refined sugar. In a small saucepan, heat the wine over low heat so that the sugar will melt when you whisk it in, making sure not to boil. Carefully whisk in the sugar then remove from the heat and let cool. "Lasts damn near forever sealed in the fridge," says Katz.

Danielle's Margarita

"I just personally love a Partida Añejo Tommy's Marg served over a big rock." 2 ounces Partida Añejo tequila, 1 ounce fresh lime juice, and ½ ounce agave nectar. Add all the ingredients to a shaker filled with ice, shake, then strain over a large ice cube into a double rocks glass. Garnish with a lime wheel.

Big
RIVER

BY CHRISTIAAN RÖLLICH FOR
FAT OX IN SCOTTSDALE, ARIZONA

1½ ounces mezcal

1½ ounces pineapple juice

1 ounce fresh lime juice

1 ounce red harissa syrup
(recipe follows)

2 dried pineapple ring halves
and 2 pineapple fronds

When Christiaan Röllich, author of *Bar Chef*, ran the bar programs for Suzanne Goin and Caroline Styne's Los Angeles restaurants—AOC, Tavern, and Lucques—he made a lot of the cocktail ingredients himself. Röllich crafted cocktails like a chef building a dish, using seasonal produce for bitters, liqueurs, and even bathtub gin. Doing so allowed him to seize control of the cocktail's flavors and put his own stamp on his riffs on classics. He credits Goin for the inspiration to use harissa. "She used it a lot in her dishes, so I tried changing it into a syrup, and it came out wonderful," he says. "The exotic fruits mixed with North African flavors and mezcal. It's an awesome cocktail."

Add the mezcal, pineapple juice, lime juice, and harissa syrup to a shaker filled with ice and shake hard for 7 seconds. Strain over fresh ice in a double rocks glass. Garnish with dried pineapple ring halves and pineapple fronds.

RED HARISSA SYRUP

Make rich simple syrup by stirring 3 cups of sugar into 2 cups of water until the sugar is dissolved. "Because of the bell peppers, the syrup becomes a little lighter, so I had to adjust the ratio a bit," says Röllich. Separate out 2 cups of the rich simple syrup and add 1 chopped, seeded red bell pepper, 1 teaspoon cumin, 1 teaspoon caraway, 1 teaspoon coriander, 1 teaspoon black pepper, 1 teaspoon turmeric, and ½ teaspoon saffron. The syrup will keep for 3 to 4 days in the refrigerator.

Christiaan's Margarita

1½ ounces reposado tequila, 1 ounce fresh lime juice, 1 ounce fresh orange juice, and 2½ teaspoons white sugar. Add all the ingredients in a short shaker, stir until the sugar is dissolved, and fill with ice. Shake hard for 7 seconds, then strain over fresh ice into a double rocks glass. Finish with two straws and a lime wedge on a cocktail spear.

Clarified
MARGARITA

BY MAX REIS FOR GRACIAS MADRE
IN WEST HOLLYWOOD

2 ounces blanco tequila

1¼ ounces clarified lime cordial
(recipe follows)

2 dashes orange bitters

Lime peel for expressing

When Max Reis ran the bar program at vegan Mexican restaurant Gracias Madre in 2016, he started experimenting with centrifugal clarification, creating clarified lime juice to stir into a Tommy's Margarita. Why clarify lime juice? Reis found that not only was this a zero-waste ingredient—he uses day-old juice and discarded peels from the limes used the night before—but it allowed the tequila (or mezcal) to shine. This is a more advanced recipe, but it's delicious!

Add the tequila, clarified lime cordial, and orange bitters to a mixing glass filled with ice, stir to chill, then strain over a large ice cube in a rocks glass, or serve up. Express a lime peel over the glass and discard.

CLARIFIED LIME CORDIAL

Max's process does require 4¼ cups of lime juice, which, when made into a cordial, can make about 40 cocktails and extends the clarified lime's shelf life from less than a week to several months. Begin by making the clarified lime. In a bowl, add ½ teaspoon Pectinex and ½ teaspoon Kieselsol (both are available online at modernistpantry.com) to 4¼ cups lime juice and stir to combine. Let rest for 15 minutes then add ½ teaspoon Chitosan to the mixture and stir to combine. Let rest for 15 minutes then add another ½ teaspoon Kieselsol to the mixture and stir to combine. Let rest for 20 minutes. When the solids and the liquids separate, rack off or syphon the clarified liquid from the top of the lime juice, being careful to not reintegrate the solids into the clarified liquid. Discard the solids. To make the cordial, add 4¼ cups clarified lime juice, 5 cups sugar, ¼ cup plus 3 tablespoons lime peel, 1½ tablespoons lime acid (2 parts citric acid to 1 part malic acid), and ¾ teaspoon salt to a pot over medium heat, stirring, until the liquid begins to steam and the sugar is dissolved. Remove from the heat and let the cordial mixture rest for 2 hours then double strain. The cordial will keep for up to 1 month in the refrigerator, but you can add 1 ounce of high-proof neutral grain spirit to extend its shelf life.

Baby TURTLE

BY THE TEAM AT TRICK DOG
IN SAN FRANCISCO

2 ounces reposado tequila,
preferably Tequila Ocho

¾ ounce fresh lime juice

¾ ounce egg white

½ ounce grapefruit juice

½ ounce cassia syrup
(recipe follows)

¼ ounce Campari

10 drops 20 percent saline
solution (page 149)

Cinnamon stick for grated garnish

Although Josh Harris, founder of James Beard–nominated bar Trick Dog, says he wouldn't call this cocktail a margarita, one can't help but recognize elements of the classic recipe in its makeup, with Campari standing in for the orange liqueur. "It's a tequila citrus drink that's delicious," he says plainly. The Baby Turtle is a beloved Trick Dog classic, having first appeared on the bar's opening menu, the Pantone menu, in 2014. Even after a decade and eighteen menu changes, people still walk into the bar and request it. Fortunately, the bar always has the ingredients on hand to make it.

Add the tequila, lime juice, egg white, grapefruit juice, cassia syrup, Campari, and saline solution to a shaker and dry shake (without ice). Fill the shaker with ice and shake until chilled. Double strain into a double rocks glass over ice and grate a cinnamon stick over it.

CASSIA SYRUP

In a small pot over medium heat, add 4 cups of white sugar to 2 cups of water. Stir until the sugar completely dissolves. Crush 50 grams of cassia sticks and add them to the pot. Bring to a boil, cover, and take it off the heat. Allow to infuse for 20 minutes. Strain out the cassia and store the syrup in a glass jar. It will keep in the refrigerator for 2 weeks.

Josh's NA Margarita

2 ounces Almave blanco, ½ ounce fresh lime juice, ¼ ounce agave nectar, and 3 dashes of All the Bitter alcohol-free orange bitters. Using a lime, wet a thick one-quarter section of the rim of a rocks glass, apply black sea salt, and set aside. Add all the ingredients to a shaker filled with ice, shake, then double strain over fresh ice into the rocks glass. Garnish with a dehydrated lime wheel.

Dat Purple
MARG

HIBISCUS CHILE MARGARITA

BY RAMSEY MUSK FOR MA'AM SIR
IN LOS ANGELES

1 ounce blanco tequila, preferably
El Tesoro, or mezcal, preferably
La Luna or Mal Bien

¾ ounce Cointreau

¼ ounce Chareau

¾ ounce fresh lime juice

¾ ounce mixed chile Jamaica
syrup (recipe follows)

Absinthe for rim and garnish

Bay leaf salt (recipe follows)
or Tajín for rim

Edible orchid or dehydrated lime
wheel for garnish

What started as a way to use up excess produce from the kitchen turned into a hit cocktail for barman Ramsey Musk, who first created this purple margarita for the now-closed Filipino restaurant Ma'am Sir in Los Angeles. "I mean, hibiscus, chile, and cucumber in LA?! Shocker," he says. This cocktail has followed him in different iterations to his subsequent bar programs at Guerrilla Tacos and Causita. "It is such a simple stunner that really fits every palate, so I am stoked it's so well received."

Rim a rocks glass with absinthe, dip in bay leaf salt, and set aside (see page 23). Add the tequila or mezcal, Cointreau, Chareau, lime juice, and chile Jamaica syrup to a shaker filled with ice and shake for about 10 seconds. Strain over ice into the prepared glass. Garnish with a spray of absinthe and an edible orchid or dehydrated lime wheel.

MIXED CHILE JAMAICA SYRUP

Cut 2 serrano peppers, 1 jalapeño pepper, and 1 poblano pepper in half, leaving the seeds. Add them to a pot along with 4 cups sugar, 3½ cups water, and ¾ cup plus 2 tablespoons dried hibiscus and bring to a boil. Remove from the heat, strain, and refrigerate. The syrup will keep in the refrigerator for 1 to 2 weeks.

BAY LEAF SALT

Add 1 cup salt, ½ cup plus 1 tablespoon black pepper, and 1¼ cups dried bay leaves to a blender and blend on high for 30 seconds.

MARGUERITE

BY ADAM FOURNIER FOR SPAGO
IN BEVERLY HILLS, CALIFORNIA

2 ounces apricot-infused
nonalcoholic agave spirit
(recipe follows)

1 ounce hibiscus sec
(recipe follows)

¾ ounce fresh lime juice

Scant ¼ ounce agave nectar

Lime wedge and kosher salt
for rim

As the first-ever bar director of Wolfgang Puck's flagship restaurant, Spago Beverly Hills, Adam Fournier is tasked with bringing the 40-year-old icon up to speed with current cocktail trends by creating a bar program with compelling culinary cocktails as well as spirit-free drinks. Not only does he build a flavorful and compelling alcohol-free libation but he also carefully considers the presentation and ritual that go along with drinking. This zero-proof margarita is an exercise in that philosophy, tantalizing the tongue with notes of stone fruit, baking spices, and cranberry-like tartness. Although its specs are that of the traditional margarita, it's made with an apricot-infused nonalcoholic tequila alternative as well as what Fournier calls a hibiscus sec. He "wanted to give it a unique spin by introducing an element of agua fresca–style drinks with the hibiscus."

Rim a rocks glass with salt and set aside (see page 23). Combine all the ingredients in a shaker with ice and shake until chilled. Double strain over a large cube in the prepared glass.

APRICOT-INFUSED NONALCOHOLIC AGAVE SPIRIT

Combine 1¼ cups dried apricots and 3 cups nonalcoholic agave spirit (such as Lyre's) in an airtight container. Allow to infuse for 24 hours. Strain through a fine-mesh strainer into a bottle. The spirit will keep in the refrigerator for up to 3 weeks.

HIBISCUS SEC

Cut 5 oranges into quarters, including the peels, and place in an airtight container along with 2⅓ cups water, 2¼ cups sugar, 2 cloves, 1 crushed cinnamon stick, and ½ teaspoon vanilla extract. Seal and refrigerate for 24 hours. Double strain the mixture. Gently press on the fruit to extract the juice. Add 1¼ cups dried hibiscus and allow it to infuse for 20 to 25 minutes, depending on the desired taste. Then double strain out the hibiscus. The hibiscus sec will keep in a glass container in the refrigerator for up to 3 weeks.

Iconic
ITERATIONS

Primo
MARGARITA

BY TONY ABOU-GANIM FOR
HARRY DENTON'S STARLIGHT
ROOM IN SAN FRANCISCO

2 ounces blanco tequila

1 ounce Cointreau

2 ounces lemon sour
(recipe follows)

1 ounce fresh lime juice

Lime wedge for garnish

The Modern Mixologist author Tony Abou-Ganim is behind many important modern cocktail moments, from creating the modern classic Cable Car cocktail to putting Julio Bermejo and his iconic Tommy's Margarita on the map. But in 1998 the cocktail pioneer created his own celebrated take on the margarita by adding lemon sour, which he says "brings another layer of sharpness." The Primo has followed him to every bar program he's worked on, from Harry Denton's Starlight Room in San Francisco to Las Vegas's Allegiant Stadium, where they sell between 7,000 and 9,000 Primo Margaritas a night. And even with the high volume of margaritas there, Abou-Ganim makes sure that every one is made with fresh, hand-squeezed lime juice as well as Cointreau. "I'm probably responsible for more Cointreau depletions in the United States than any bartender walking the face of the planet, but I insist on it," he says.

Add the tequila, Cointreau, lemon sour, and lime juice to a shaker filled with ice and shake until chilled. Strain into a Collins glass over fresh ice. Garnish with a lime wedge.

LEMON SOUR

Mix 2 parts fresh lemon juice with 1 part light agave syrup (page 149). The sour will keep in the refrigerator for up to 3 days.

Tony's Margarita

"I just make the Tommy's Margarita. I'll do a 1:1 light agave syrup [page 149], equal parts fresh lime with two parts of my favorite tequila. My go-to is always going to be blanco. I want to taste the agave."

Salt Air
MARGARITA

BY CHEF JOSÉ ANDRÉS FOR CAFÉ
ATLÁNTICO IN WASHINGTON, D.C.

1½ ounces tequila

¾ ounce Combier

1 ounce fresh lime juice

1 ounce simple syrup (page 149)

4 tablespoons salt air
(recipe follows) for garnish

The origin story behind this margarita is poetic and almost romantic. For celebrity chef and World Central Kitchen founder José Andrés, the idea of adding "salt air" to a margarita came to him when he was sitting on the beach in Andalucía, Spain, with his wife, Tichi. As they watched the waves crash on the shore, he wondered about "how light and salty those waves would taste on your lips." The idea of using foams and air wasn't new to him as he worked with them at innovative haute cuisine restaurant El Bulli, but he had never created a salt air. And what better place to try it for the first time than on a margarita? "I think this salty foam feels so much more natural [than crunchy salt]," he says. Andrés first served the Salt Air Margarita in 2002 at his Latin-inspired restaurant, Café Atlántico in Washington, D.C., where it was an immediate hit. The cocktail has since gone on to become one of the most requested cocktails at his restaurants.

Add the tequila, Combier, lime juice, and simple syrup to a shaker filled with ice and shake vigorously. Strain into a chilled cocktail glass. Garnish with salt air and serve immediately.

SALT AIR

Combine 1 cup water and 1 teaspoon sucrose esters (available online at modernistpantry.com) in a small saucepan. Heat the mixture on low until it reaches at least 158°F, whisking constantly to activate the sucrose esters. (If you don't have a thermometer, simply cook the mixture until it starts to bubble.) Remove from the heat and cool the saucepan in an ice bath. Once cool, add ½ cup fresh lime juice and 2 tablespoons kosher salt. With an immersion blender, blend the mixture until it begins to foam up. Once the whole mixture is foamy, it's ready to spoon atop the cocktail. The mixture will keep in an airtight container for up to 3 days in the refrigerator.

The
INFANTE

BY GIUSEPPE GONZÁLEZ
FOR FLATIRON LOUNGE
IN NEW YORK CITY

2 ounces blanco tequila

¾ ounce fresh lime juice

¾ ounce orgeat

2 dashes rose water

Freshly ground nutmeg
for garnish

Back in 2006, when Giuseppe González was the head bartender at Julie Reiner's trailblazing Flatiron Lounge, Jill DeGroff, artist and wife of cocktail legend Dale DeGroff, asked González to share a cocktail for her book, *Lush Life: Portraits from the Bar.* "This is literally my favorite tequila drink I had invented," González says. Being the type of bartender who has a habit of trying to improve recipes—look what he did for the Jungle Bird—he streamlined Trader Vic's Pinky Gonzales, basically a Mai Tai that swaps out the rum for tequila. Looking at the 1972 recipe, he broke it down to what he believed was its most important element: orgeat. "If you're using high-quality orgeat, you're good. If you're using some bullshit that's super medicinal and tastes kind of pharmaceutical, like artificially flavored almond, it's just not going to pop the way real orgeat fucking does."

Add the tequila, lime juice, orgeat, and rose water to a shaker filled with ice and shake until chilled. Strain over a large ice cube into a rocks glass. Garnish with a sprinkling of freshly ground nutmeg across the top.

Giuseppe's Margarita

Tommy's specs with Fortaleza or G4 tequila or Código or Ojo de Tigre mezcal.

Rhode ISLAND RED

BY VINCENZO MARIANELLA FOR
PROVIDENCE IN LOS ANGELES

2 ounces blanco tequila

¾ ounce Chambord

¾ ounce fresh lemon juice

¼ ounce agave nectar

1 dash orange bitters

2 ounces ginger beer

Lemon and lime twists for garnish

At this point, I like to think the margarita template just floats in the collective consciousness, inspiring people without their knowing it. Such is the case with Vincenzo Marianella and his Rhode Island Red, which *Los Angeles Magazine* named "Best Summer Cocktail of 2005." The imposing but charming 6'4" Italian barman is credited with introducing farmers' market–fresh cocktails to Los Angeles through his game-changing program at Michelin-starred restaurant Providence in 2005. The Rhode Island Red debuted on its opening menu. When asked if the margarita was the source of inspiration for it, he replied, "Not really, it was inspired by summer in California." But one can see the bones of the traditional margarita in the recipe. "I was looking for a summer cocktail, and tequila was kind of new for me," he explains. "So it looks like a good idea, and I started playing around."

Add the tequila, Chambord, lemon juice, agave nectar, and bitters to a shaker filled with ice and shake until chilled. Strain into an ice-filled Collins glass. Top with ginger beer and garnish with lemon and lime twists.

Vincenzo's Margarita

2 ounces blanco tequila, ¾ ounce fresh lime juice, and "a very shy 1 ounce of 1:1 agave syrup" (page 149).

Syrups, Super Juice, and Salts

Agave syrup: For 1:1, mix 1 part agave nectar with 1 part warm (but not boiling) water. For 2:1, mix 2 parts agave nectar with 1 part warm (but not boiling) water. For 3:1, it's 3 parts agave nectar and 1 part warm (but not boiling) water. Stir until thoroughly combined. The syrup will keep in an airtight container in the refrigerator for up to 3 weeks or in the freezer for up to 6 months.

Chile salt (Max Reis): Add ¼ cup of powdered chipotle chile (or chile powder of your choice), 1 cup of kosher salt (or fine sea salt), and 1 tablespoon of white sugar (optional) to a container and stir to combine. If the chile is too spicy, the sugar will dampen the heat.

Lime super juice: Thoroughly wash 8 to 12 limes and peel. Combine the peels (about 1 to 1½ cups of lime peels) with 5½ teaspoons of powdered citric acid and 2 teaspoons of powdered malic acid. Allow the mixture to sit at room temperature for about an hour. "Once the acid is dissolved into fluid, it's good to go," explains super juice creator Nickle Morris. "Lime peels will begin to brown. Keep an eye on that." In the meantime, juice the limes and set the juice aside. After an hour, add 4¼ cups of cold water to the acid mixture, place in a blender, and blend. Strain into a sealable container. To make the lime super juice, mix the oleo citrate with the lime juice until combined. The super juice will keep in an airtight container in the refrigerator for up to 2 weeks.

10 percent saline solution: In a mason jar combine 1 heaping tablespoon kosher salt with 7 tablespoons filtered water and mix until the salt dissolves.

20 percent saline solution: In a mason jar combine 2 heaping tablespoons kosher salt with 7 tablespoons filtered water and mix until the salt dissolves.

Simple syrup: For 1:1, mix 1 part sugar with 1 part warm (but not boiling) water. For 2:1, aka rich simple syrup, mix 2 parts sugar to 1 part water. Combine by shaking them in a mason jar or a shaker, or by using a blender. By keeping it off the stove, you're getting the most neutral version of this sweetener. Cooking it will add flavors and make your cocktail sweeter.

Acknowledgments

I'm indebted to all the bartenders and torchbearers who generously shared their recipes and stories with me and patiently answered all my questions and follow-up questions: Jean Michel Alperin, Eric Alperin, Benjamin Amberg, Chef José Andrés, Natasha Bermudez, Matthew Biancaniello, Pam Blanton, Chris Bostick, Beau du Bois, Andrew Burton, José Medina Camacho, Erick Castro, Adam Chase, Demi Close, Patrick Connolly, Julian Cox, Kristina Cox, Danielle Crouch, Sarah Crowl, Britta Currie, Natasha David, John deBary, Kevin Diedrich, Trevor Easter, William Elliott, Daniel Eun, Simon Ford, Adam Fournier, Giuseppe González, Kim Haasarud, John Hardin, Josh Harris, the Trick Dog team, Allan Katz, Lukas Kaufmann, the 28 HongKong Street team, Sherra Kurtz, Justin Lavenue, Jen Len, Bricia Lopez, Vincenzo Marianella, Lynnette Marrero, José Luis León Martinez, Paul McGee, Julia McKinley, Emily Mistell, Ivy Mix, Jeffrey Morgenthaler, Ramsey Musk, Shannon Mustipher, Vince Ott, Joshua Perry, Heather Potts, Jazzton Rodriguez, Christiaan Röllich, Abigail Smith, Kim Stodel, Christian Suzuki-Orellana, Stacey Swenson, Paul Taylor, Sother Teague, Travis Tober, Tad Tobey, Chockie Tom, Ivan Vasquez, Stuart Weaver, Christine Wiseman, and Alex Zeichner. Cheers to David Cordoba, Ellen Kruce, Benjamin Padrón, Kevin Williamson, and Phil Ward for creating everlasting margarita-inspired masterpieces.

Huge thanks to Elmy Bermejo for connecting me with Julio Bermejo and making sure he stopped by Tommy's when I made the trek to San Francisco to see him. And Julio, it was such an honor to sit at your bar and have you walk me through how different tequilas taste in a Tommy's Margarita. I may not have finished all eight of them, but I loved and appreciated the moment.

Tony Abou-Ganim, thanks for sharing your recipe as well as your stories from when you first met Julio and how he blew you away with his Tommy's Margarita to when you first tasted a 100 percent agave tequila while doing a shot with Boz Scaggs in 1986.

Dave Arnold, thanks for taking the time to recheck your Cape Cod Margarita recipe—even though I ultimately went with the Booker & Dax marg. Shout out to your assistant, Quinn, for making sure my questions got answered as well.

Max Reis, you are always so patient with my many texted questions and requests. And even though I originally wanted an easy version of your clarified margarita, you reminded me that it's better to do something right, something that takes more work, than shortcut it to something mediocre.

My fellow bloggers and authors Gaby Mlynarczyk and Natalie Bovis, I don't even know if you have ever met each other, but you were both there for me when I was first offered this book and was so nervous about taking it on. You each gave me the "atta girl" that I needed. And thanks for sharing your recipes!

Karen Foley at *Imbibe* magazine, thanks for the opportunity and for allowing me to experience what it feels like to actually be excited about my job.

Talia Baiocchi, I'm so grateful and humbled that you passed my name along to Ten Speed Press to write this book. You made my dream come true.

My book editor, Kim Keller! You don't know how happy you made me when you first reached out to ask if I'd be interested in writing a book about margaritas for my dream publisher. It's been such a pleasure working with you. You made it all so fun and possible.

Of course, this beautiful book would never have come to fruition or caught anyone's eye without the team at Ten Speed Press: production designer Mari Gill, production editor Sohayla Farman, copy editor Amy Kovalski, production manager Philip Leung, associate director of marketing Stephanie Davis, marketing manager Andrea Portanova, and publicist Natalie Yera-Campbell.

Many thanks to art director (and rock star) Emma Campion, photographer Leela Cyd, and cocktail maker Carrie Purcell. Your vision, creativity, and skills have made this book—and margaritas—so beautiful. I'll always cherish the memories of our Santa Barbara shoot days.

My siblings, Jennifer and Gerard, you were my first muses, writing partners, and editors. My mom and dad, Esther and Efren, you both instilled in me a sense of adventure, a love of exploring, and a penchant for hosting parties. My brothers-in-law Chris Vosse and David Sedgwick, cheers for making my brother and sister so happy and for your support. My niece, Astrid, even though you're eleven now, I did this book for you, too, so you can see what's possible.

Jay Kavanagh—my favorite travel companion, drinking buddy, and official margarita taster—I, for sure, wouldn't have been able to do this without you. Your love, belief in me, and support empowered and continue to empower me.

Index

A

Abou-Ganim, Tony, 5, 9, 10, 127, 141
acid, 11–12, 14
Adiós Margarita, 31
agave nectar, 15–16
agave syrup, 16, 149
Alperin, Eric and Jean Michel, 35
Amberg, Benjamin, 126
Andrés, José, 142
Arnold, Dave, 12, 15, 28, 69

B

Baby Turtle, 132, *133*
Baller's Margarita, 60, *61*
barware, 18, 20
Bergeron, Victor (Trader Vic), 22, 32, 101, 145
Bermejo, Julio, 5, 30, 141
Bermudez, Natasha, 45
Biancaniello, Matthew, 84
Big River, 128, *129*
Black Forest Margarita, 80
Blended Strawberry Margarita, 56
blender tips, 17, 18
BLT Margarita, 124–25, *125*
Boogie Nights, 64–65, *65*
Booker & Dax Blender Margarita, 69
Bostick, Chris, 95
Bovis, Natalie, 105
Bruce Banner, 90–91, *91*
Buffett, Jimmy, 4
Bullock, Tim, 35
Burton, Andrew, 71

C

Camacho, José Medina, 31
Castro, Erick, 5, 20, 60
chile peppers, 25
chile salt, 149
Christmas Margarita, *104,* 105
Clarified Margarita, *130,* 131
Classic Margarita, 28, *29*
Close, Demi, 51
Coconut Margarita, 81
Cointreau, 14
Collins, Brendan, 101
Combier, 15
Cordoba, David, 68
Cox, Julian, 28, 90, 91
Crouch, Danielle, 127
Crowl, Sarah, 124, 125
curaçao, 15
Currie, Britta, 78

D

Dat Purple Marg, *134,* 135
David, Natasha, 93
The Day After the Day of the Dead, 84, *85*
deBary, John, 42
DeGroff, Dale, 5, 11, 127, 145
DeGroff, Jill, 145
Denton, Harry, 141
Diedrich, Kevin, 21, 59
Dirty Marg-tini, *50,* 51
du Bois, Beau, 81

E

Easter, Trevor, 78
Ehrmann, H. Joseph, 18
Elliott, William, 110
El Morado, 101
Eun, Daniel, 54

F

50/50 Margarita, *44,* 45
Foolish Pleasures, *58,* 59
Ford, Simon, 41
Fournier, Adam, 136
Friedland, Jonathan, 5
Frozen Jägerita, 68
Frozen Margarita, 36

G

garnishes, 23
Georgia O'Keeffe, 114, *115*

glassware, 22
Goin, Suzanne, 128
González, Giuseppe, 145
Gram-arita Cadillac Margarita Batch, *34,* 35
Grand Marnier, 15

H

Haasarud, Kim, 6, 80
Hail Mary, 54, *55*
Hang Loose Brah, *82,* 83
Hardin, John, 21, 102
Harris, Josh, 132
Hayworth, Rita, 1
Herrera, Carlos "Danny," 1
Heugel, Bobby, 124
Hibiscus Margarita, 38, *39*
Hilton, Conrad "Nicky," Jr., 2
Hocus Pocus, 127

I

ice, 17
The Infante, *144,* 145

J

Jägerita, Frozen, 68
juicing, 12, 20

K

Katz, Allan, 127
Kaufmann, Lukas, 117
King, Marjorie, 1
Kruce, Ellen, 48
Kurtz, Sherra, 67

L

Lagerita, 41
Lavenue, Justine, 77
Len, Jen, 114
Lieberman, Theo, 20
lime super juice, 149
Lonesome Rose Margarita, 32, *33*
Lopez, Bricia, 25, 100
Low Altitude, 93

M

Madre Mezcal
    Margarita, 37
Maison Margarita de
    Jamaica, 110, *111*
Malcriada, 106, *107*
Mano a Mango, 74, *75*
Mano de Chango,
    122, *123*
Margarita Al Pastor,
    112, 113
margaritas
    garnishing, 23
    glass for, 22
    key ingredients for,
        9–12, 14–16
    origins of, 1–2
    popularity of, 2, 4–5
    spicing up, 21, 22, 25
    variations on, 5–7
    See also individual
        recipes
Margarita Toreada, 100
Margarita Verde, 96, *97*
Marguerite, 136, *137*
Marianella, Vincenzo, 146
Marrero, Lynnette, 74
Martinez, Mariano, 5, 36
McGee, Paul, 28, 32
McKinley, Julia, 32
Méndeza, Jesús, 31
Mexican Martini, 48
Miller, Alex, 4
Mistell, Emily, 56, 57
Mix, Ivy, 6, 21, 109
mixes, 16, 18
Mlynarczyk, Gaby, 101
Morales, Pancho, 2
Morgenthaler, Jeffrey,
    12, 68, 126
Morris, Nickle, 14
Murphy, Heather, 5
Musk, Ramsey, 135
Mustipher, Shannon, 38
Myers, David, 90

O

Oaxacan Sunrise,
    56–57, *57*
orange liqueurs, 14–15
Ott, Vince, 6, 64, 65

P

Padrón, Benjamin, 113
Parsons, Gram, 35
Picante Amante, 102, *103*
Podracer, 92
Potts, Heather, 48
Primo Margarita,
    140, 141
Puck, Wolfgang, 136

R

Ranch Water, 40
Red Zeppelin, *88,* 89
Reiner, Julie, 11,
    127, 145
Reis, Max, 17, 21, 23, 52,
    53, 131, 149
Retox, 49
Rhode Island Red,
    146, *147*
rim, salting, 22–23
Rodriguez, Jazzton, 51
Röllich, Christiaan, 128
Ross, Sam, 5, 90

S

salt, 22–23, 149
Salt Air Margarita,
    142, *143*
Sames, Margaret
    "Margarita," 2
Sanschagrin, Grover, 9
Scoville scale, 25
shaking methods, 20
simple syrup, 16, 149
Singer, Daniel, 18
Sí Punch, 52–53, *53*
Smells Like Teen Spirit,
    42, *43*
Smith, Abigail, 89
Sonámbula, *108,* 109
Southbound
    Suarez, 126
Spa Day Margarita,
    94, 95
Stipe, Katie, 127
Stodel, Kim, 20, 122
Strawberry Margarita,
    Super, 78, *79*
Styne, Caroline, 128
Summer Melon Marg,
    70, 71

Super Strawberry
    Margarita, 78, *79*
Suzuki-Orellana,
    Christian, 106
sweeteners, 15–16
Swenson, Stacey, 96
syrups, 149

T

Taylor, Paul, 67
Teague, Sother, 49
tequilas, 9–11
Tober, Travis, 17, 36
Tom, Chockie, 121
Tommy's Amontillado,
    66, 67
Tommy's Margarita, 30
Trader Vic. *See*
    Bergeron, Victor
Trick Dog, 132
triple sec, 14
28 Guava Spicy
    Margarita, *116,* 117
28 HongKong Street,
    68, 117

V

Vasquez, Ivan, 6, 37
Vast Acid Margarita,
    120, 121
Voltaggio, Michael, 101

W

Wachtel, April, 18
Ward, Phil, 37
Waterloo Watermelon
    Margarita, *76,* 77
Weaver, Stuart, 92
Williamson, Kevin, 40
Wiseman, Christine, 83
Wondrich, David, 2

Y

Yu, Justin, 124

Published in the United States by Ten Speed Press, an imprint of Random House, a division of Penguin Random House LLC, New York.
TenSpeed.com

Ten Speed Press and the Ten Speed Press colophon are registered trademarks of Penguin Random House LLC.

For further information on the sources used in this book, please visit www.carolinepardilla.com/margarita-time-bibliography.

Typefaces: Fontsmith's FS Elliot, Melvastype's Handelson, Monotype's Posterama 1901, and ParaType's Vaccine

Library of Congress Cataloging-in-Publication Data is on file with the publisher.

Hardcover ISBN: 978-1-9848-6294-5
eBook ISBN: 978-1-9848-6295-2

Printed in China

Acquiring editor: Kim Keller | Production editor: Sohayla Farman
Art director: Emma Campion | Production designer: Mari Gill
Production manager: Phil Leung
Drink stylist: Carrie Purcell | Food stylist assistant: Liza Saragosa
Photo assistants: David Kilpatrick and Siena Perez Del Campo
Models: Siena Perez Del Campo, Ian Gamblin, Megan Nayar, Tenzin Yega
Copyeditor: Amy Kovalski | Proofreaders: Eldes Tran and Alison Kerr Miller
Indexer: Ken DellaPenta
Publicist: Natalie Yera-Campbell | Marketer: Andrea Portnova

10 9 8 7 6 5 4 3 2 1

First Edition

"In *Margarita Time*, Caroline Pardilla applies her keen trendspotting eye to the margarita. She offers a deep dive into what the drink looks like today and how top pros around the world are shaping the world's most popular cocktail. No matter how well you think you know the marg, expect to find a few surprises in these pages. I know I did."

—Kara Newman, author of *Cocktails with a Twist*, *Nightcap*, and *Shake. Stir. Sip.*

"Few cocktails are more deserving of book-length treatment than the mighty margarita, which year in and year out reigns as one of the world's most popular drinks, and few writers are more equipped to take you on a tour of the multifarious marg world than seasoned surveyor of the cocktail demimonde, Caroline Pardilla."

—Robert Simonson, author of *A Proper Drink* and creator of the award-nominated Substack newsletter *The Mix with Robert Simonson*

"Informal surveys of the glasses scattered along random bartops are likely to reveal the same thing: The margarita's time is now. In *Margarita Time*, Caroline Pardilla starts with the simple basics of this classic cocktail then takes us all on the grand tour through its many impressive incarnations."

—Paul Clarke, editor in chief of *Imbibe* and host of the *Radio Imbibe* podcast

"With *Margarita Time*, Caroline Pardilla has gone the extra mile in sourcing a thirst-inducing collection of recipes from the industry's best and brightest bartenders. Whether you're a casual cocktail drinker or a serious agave nerd, this book will be a reliable go-to for years to come."

—Emma Janzen, award-winning spirits and cocktail journalist and author of *Mezcal: The History, Craft & Cocktails of the World's Ultimate Artisanal Spirit*